Living Off Landscape

GLOBAL AESTHETIC RESEARCH

Series editor:

Joseph J. Tanke, associate professor, Department of Philosophy, University of Hawaii

The Global Aesthetic Research series publishes cutting-edge research in the field of aesthetics. It contains books that explore the principles at work in our encounters with art and nature, that interrogate the foundations of artistic, literary, and cultural criticism, and that articulate the theory of the discipline's central concepts.

Titles in the Series

Early Modern Aesthetics, J. Colin McQuillan
Foucault on the Arts and Letters: Perspectives for the 21st Century, Catherine M. Soussloff
Architectural and Urban Reflections after Deleuze and Guattari, edited by Constantin V. Boundas and Vana Tentokali
Living Off Landscape: or the Unthought-of in Reason, François Jullien, translated by Pedro Rodríguez

Living Off Landscape

or the Unthought-of in Reason

François Jullien, Translated by Pedro Rodríguez

London • New York

Published by Rowman & Littlefield International Ltd
Unit A, Whitacre Mews, 26-34 Stannary Street, London SE11 4AB
www.rowmaninternational.com

Rowman & Littlefield International Ltd. is an affiliate of Rowman & Littlefield
4501 Forbes Boulevard, Suite 200, Lanham, Maryland 20706, USA
With additional offices in Boulder, New York, Toronto (Canada), and Plymouth (UK)
www.rowman.com

This translation copyright © 2018 Rowman & Littlefield International

Originally published in French as *Vivre de paysage ou L'impensé de la Raison*
Copyright © Éditions Gallimard, *Vivre de paysage ou L'impensé de la Raison*

All rights reserved. No part of this book may be reproduced in any form or by any electronic or mechanical means, including information storage and retrieval systems, without written permission from the publisher, except by a reviewer, who may quote passages in a review.

British Library Cataloguing in Publication Data

A catalogue record for this book is available from the British Library

ISBN: HB 978-1-78660-337-1
        PB 978-1-78660-338-8

Library of Congress Cataloging-in-Publication Data

Names: Jullien, François, 1951– author.
Title: Living off landscape : or, the unthought-of in reason / François Jullien ; translated by Pedro Rodriguez.
Other titles: Vivre de paysage. English
Description: Lanham : Rowman & Littlefield International, 2018. | Series: Global aesthetic research | Includes bibliographical references and index.
Identifiers: LCCN 2017045958 (print) | LCCN 2017054666 (ebook) | ISBN 9781786603395 (Electronic) | ISBN 9781786603371 (cloth : alk. paper) | ISBN 9781786603388 (pbk.).
Subjects: LCSH: Landscapes. | Philosophy, Chinese. | Aesthetics, Chinese.
Classification: LCC BH301.L3 (ebook) | LCC BH301.L3 J84513 2018 (print) | DDC 111/.85—dc23
LC record available at https://lccn.loc.gov/2017045958

∞™ The paper used in this publication meets the minimum requirements of American National Standard for Information Sciences—Permanence of Paper for Printed Library Materials, ANSI/NISO Z39.48-1992.

Printed in the United States of America

for E.L.

Contents

Prologue		ix
I	Land—Landscape: Expanse, View, Cutoff	1
II	"Mountain(s)-Water(s)"	15
III	From a Landscape to Living	27
IV	When the Perceptual Turns Out to Be Affectual	41
V	When "Spirit" Emanates from the Physical	53
VI	Tension-Setting	67
VII	Singularization, Variation, Remove	83
VIII	Connivance	105
Epilogue		123
Index		127
About the Author and Translator		135

Prologue

We can pause before the landscape as before a "spectacle": a *spectaculum*, as Petrarch called it from the heights of Mount Ventoux. We can look upon it from a "point of view," take in its harmony and variety, admire its composition, and perhaps, on closer inspection, discern some underlying geometry. We can also scan the delimiting horizon, play the "observer," and sweep our gaze over the panorama, declaring, "How lovely!" and be on our way.

But a landscape can be something else entirely.

It can draw us into the ceaseless play of its correlations and stir our vitality with its various tensions. It can awaken our sense of existence through what singularizes within it. A landscape's *remove* [*lointain*]—its sense of the faraway—feeds our reveries and lulls us into "dreaminess." In a landscape the perceptual becomes affectual. The physicality of things turns evasive and suffuses with an infinite beyond. The *divide* [écart][1] between the sensible and the spiritual is sealed at last. For a landscape ceases to be a "corner" of the world. What is revealed instead, arising suddenly and whole, is the stuff of worlds, the stuff that gives rise to a world.

---

1. The *écart*, translated here as *divide*, is a fundamental concept in the philosophy of François Jullien. It stands in contradistinction to the notion of comparison as practiced in cultural studies (e.g., comparative literature). Rather than set cultures side by side, Jullien places them on either side of an exploratory divide, so that they can "reflect" each other. In so doing they reveal each other's biases—or, to use another of Jullien's images, they discover each other's cultural headwaters—and thus bring forth new possibilities. According to Jullien, the headwaters of a particular culture lie too far upstream to be attained with the tools that the culture itself can fashion, because of the biases that flow out of those very headwaters. [Translator's note.]

And thus, discreetly, a place becomes a link. I begin to establish a sense of *connivance* with the landscape, a sense that I can no longer take my leave.

Or that if I did take my leave the landscape would only dwell on within me. Can the word *nostalgia* fully convey this?

Landscape—to cite its two most closely associated verbs in our Western languages—ceases to be something merely to "look at" or "represent." It hooks into the vital. By hazarding the title of this book, "living *off* landscape," I use a preposition that reaches down to a more primordial kernel, that digs so far below manner or means as to dissolve the separation between the concrete and the abstract (as in that homespun French recipe for happiness: "to live on love and cool water alone"). I thereby clear the way for another possibility: that we might consider this thing called "landscape" no longer as the "part" of the land that nature "presents" to an "observer," in the ordinary definition, but as a *resource*[2] on which *living* [*vivre*][3] can indefinitely draw.

It is true that Europe has only recently become aware of landscape. It cropped up in Renaissance painting and was *promoted*[4] with the boom in representation, only to be cast aside in the twentieth century. That awareness has been rekindled today with the rise of environmentalism and ecology. In China, however, landscape-thought dawned more than a thousand years earlier and thereafter developed without interruption within the lettered class. This is a unique case. Neither the Bible nor India or Islam offers up any landscape-thought: only garden-thought. The time has come to account for what we have so far only sketched out. In particular, we must ask why China was able to develop landscape-thought so early and make it so central, and how Chinese landscape-thought might help us today to *deploy*[5] our own concept of landscape, or perhaps reconfigure it altogether.

This book, then, though perhaps premature, and as yet one of a kind, follows logically from my previous work.[6] In it I continue to pursue a

---

2. *Resource* (*ressource*) is a special term in Jullien's philosophy. The *resources* of a culture, once uncovered (from across a *divide*), are available to all persons, regardless of their culture. The very purpose of his philosophy is to dig down to cultural resources, so that they might be put to use elucidating other cultures. [Translator's note.]

3. The special term *living* (*vivre*, or *le vivre*), as developed later in the book, goes beyond the usual biological sense. It has to do with reestablishing, through landscape, what Jullien calls a primordial connection between us and the world. [Translator's note.]

4. The special term *promote*, although it retains some of the word's ordinary meaning, relates to Jullien's notion of soaring [*l'essor*]. See below. [Translator's note.]

5. Jullien uses the special term *deploy* (*déployer*) in an etymological sense, to mean unfold. See the first note in chapter 1 on the use of the word *fold*. [Translator's note.]

6. Jullien uses the term *chantier*, meaning something like "philosophical dry dock." He views all of his thought as a work in progress that will remain so for as long as he lives. A finished work, for him, is *self-satisfied* and *fixed*, and thus incapable of generating anything new, whereas a *chantier* (a site of construction or continual industry), with its steady stream of *work*, partakes of *life* and can therefore generate *the new*. [Translator's note.]

philosophy of living. I intend this not only to contrast with the "question of Being" but also to repudiate every sort of vitalism. "Landscape" here is a matter of "mountains" and "water," what we see and hear, and the play of "wind" and "light." From another angle, I also address the question of what I call *the intimate*,[7] for which landscape serves as a condenser. The intimate comes to be when the boundary is breached between an interiority and the outside. The discreet kernel that emerges, finding itself set apart, is revealed to be intensive as well. I then take a further step and consider how we might undo the self-sufficiency of the Subject, which is the dominant conceit of Western thought. The Subject took on a justifiable importance in the call for Liberty, but today it bears rethinking if we hope to pull free from the mire of its bias. By the same token, the book attempts to ground a new approach to morality: one that forgoes prescription (in the sense of commandments and obligations, which we no longer care to have) and stems instead from a qualification of experience—or, more broadly, from a promotion of existence, through which we might probe the human in its *resource*.

After all, philosophy might also, or chiefly, amount to something other than giving one's opinion on everything, taking sides at every opportunity, and preaching the good life. It might instead relate to the exploration of resources. It might relate to the diviner's art, or *source-ery*.

This book was written during two stays, in the spring of 2013, at the Fondation des Treilles, for whose hospitality I am most grateful.

There was landscape there.

---

7. Jullien has devoted a book (*De l'intime: loin du bruyant Amour*) to his notion of the intimate (*l'intime*). In his sense the intimate stands in contradistinction to love. To simplify, the intimate is quiet and exists only between two, whereas love can be theatrical and one-sided. [Translator's note.]

I

✢

Land—Landscape
Expanse, View, Cutoff

1

We had best be blunt and risk laying things out right away, without preliminaries or precautions. Otherwise, I fear we will get lost in the *established* inquiry. As vast as the literature devoted to this topic now is, perhaps no one has yet dreamed to venture back to the biases that first gave rise to our very notion of "landscape." Wary as I am, then, I wonder whether we in Europe might have begun with a bad definition of landscape, or in any case, from a definition that has thrashed, constrained, and perhaps strangled the *possibility* that landscape embodies. I wonder whether the problem isn't so much that our definition is incomplete or restrictive—for then we could always just supply the missing pieces—but that it derives from implicit choices: choices that have gelled into a system and, through their very coherence, have encumbered the deployment of the resulting thought. In other words, we as a culture have unwittingly mortgaged our landscape-thought, but to what (and how)? Like so much silt, our landscape-thought has settled into a *fold*.[1] We hope to scoop it back out, but our hope has come at the cost of serial amendments and even theoretical revolutions. Will such measures suffice?

---

1. The fold (*pli*) is a key image in Jullien's philosophy and ties in with his (etymological) use of the word *deployment*, which literally means *unfolding*. Deployed thought is thought that has had its folds smoothed out, so that whatever has fallen into the folds (fallen through the cracks, we might say in English) can partake of *living*: that is, can exercise its generative power. [Translator's note.]

To put a finer point on the initial difficulty, we might ask whether these *implicit choices* or biases that undergird European thought, and through which it conceives what it has called "landscape," have not locked us into a certain perspective, snared us in "the obvious." Have we ever stirred from this position, and have we not as a result been led astray on the subject of landscape? The fact is, we remain stuck in a rut that we *do not see*. Europe coined the term *landscape* in the mid-sixteenth century (1549 in France). Since then the definition has languished in a strange fixity, advancing not a whit. In its most recent formulation (from the *Robert* dictionary of French) a landscape is said to be "a piece of land that nature presents to an observer."[2] But this only repeats the definition set forth at the start, four centuries ago, in which landscape is an "expanse" or "piece" of land as it "appears to the eye." It is "the look of a piece of land," in the summary of Furetière's dictionary (1690): "the territory that extends as far as the eye can see."[3]

I begin with European reason because *landscape* is a European term, an exemplary European term. The French word *paysage*, deriving from *pays*, is found in language after language, and the word's composition remains constant throughout—as if the notion could have no other point of departure and there were no imaginable way out of the semantics. In northern Europe we find *Land*—*Land-schaft* (German) and *land*—*land-scape* (English). They say "landscape" was invented in the Low Countries, so perhaps we ought to have begun with Flemish: *landschap*. To the south the Italians have their *paesaggio* and the Spaniards their *paisaje*. Even the Russians follow suit, with пейзаж. We have before us an indubitably European term: to wit, a term that sets out a theoretical geography of Europe, or a term I would say that "gives rise to Europe." If we dig down to the root we find Latin already Hellenizing things with *topiaria* (*opera*), which (in both Pliny the Elder and Vitruvius) derives from *topos*, or "place." Europe has not emerged from the idea—or the presumption, rather—that a landscape is something that the eye cuts out of a piece of "land."

It is noteworthy, too, that "landscape" was first named (thought through) with respect to painting. It is painting, we observe, that has borne landscape-thought in Europe, but in steering what course? The term *landscape* was developed by painters and for painting. It came to fruition through what was, for once, a generous exchange between northern and southern Europe: specifically, between the Flemish masters (e.g., Patinir), who brought nature from the background to the foreground, and the Italian masters, whose revolution laid down a new criterion for veracity. "Landscape" became a near tautology for "painting depicting a land-

---

2. "*La partie d'un pays que la nature présente à un observateur.*" [Translator's note.]
3. "*L'aspect d'un pays*"; "*le territoire qui s'étend jusqu'où la vue peut porter.*" [Translator's note.]

scape," and then came to refer to the pictorial genre itself. All of this—landscape's development by painters and for painting, the north-south exchange, and the shift of referent from view to artwork and then again to genre—ought to surprise us, because landscape met with centuries of reticence in Europe before it was finally established. Landscape painting was, as we know, born of a change in the art, but for a long time before then all it did was fill the "empty corners." It was background, decor. It made but slow progress in European art, wriggling free of the hegemony of "history": that is, of both the significance of "action" (Félibien) and the ideal beauty incarnate in the body (Lessing).

Though it is early yet, we should review what we know of this story. It is a story we know well—all too well, perhaps. We have so thoroughly imbibed it that we no longer think it through. Indeed, it is perhaps already symptomatic that the story should flow without a hiccup through Europe's so very gradual *adequation*[4] of painting and landscape. The delayed advent of landscape painting in Europe suggests resistance, but a resistance—let us ask—to what? In the scale of values, landscape was at first a minor genre, long subservient in academic hierarchies to the depiction of characters. (The painters themselves were in this respect more pioneering: witness Poussin and Claude Lorrain.) Not until the nineteenth century (e.g., in Turner and, to a lesser degree, Ravier) did landscape gain its independence, but it promptly fell apart right at the start of the twentieth. The new century looked askance at what we call "nature." We expected nature to be natural, but it was never free of artifice. And thus the twentieth century deliberately steered composition toward further abstraction.

In European painting, then, did landscape arise conceptually and come into its own as the mere temporary boon of a *transition*? Did it occur in the narrow window or tight niche of a scant few decades—after the close of the Romantic era, when painting tired of both the rigors of resemblance and the cult of ideal beauty, and before the way was cleared for brute sensation (or what we hoped was, at last, brute sensation) and for the indeterminacy of an elementary kernel? Did it occur before intellectual construction (or deconstruction) truly freed itself from *representation*—landscape being the final attempt at representation, or indeed the first drib to overflow the cup? Does this not *already* suggest that European painting-thought just happened to discover landscape along the way; that it sounded those depths without dropping anchor, opting instead to sail

---

4. Another key term in Jullien's philosophy, tying in with his concepts of *coincidence* and *de-coincidence*. A thing that coincides with itself, that exactly matches itself (Jullien is using both the temporal and the geometric sense of the term), has achieved self-sufficiency and therefore death. Only what de-coincides with itself, what peels away from itself, is alive. In other terms, *coincidence* is *adequation*. [Translator's note.]

on to waters farther ahead; and that in prospecting it discovered a potential seam but found no proper way to mine it—no way to exploit what I have started to call the "resource"?

2

Thus it behooves us to venture back in our thinking—or rather into our *unthought-of*—with respect to "landscape."

We arrive first at what lies nearest: "what" we think, as object, and our *cogitatum*, what our thought "happens upon": what our thought happens upon when it thinks "landscape." But we have no purchase on "what" we think, on what our thought "happens upon." We have so little initiative in this regard that we are quickly stuck with this "what." It is already resultative. Anterior to this, further upstream—and more determinative as well—is "what we think *about*": what *it occurs to us to think*. For many centuries in Europe it never occurred to us to think about landscape. We were never compelled to excise and name something on the order of "landscape" within the nonetheless ever-expanding sphere of the paintable and the thinkable. To do that we needed new stakes to arise, new perspectives to appear. We needed new tools with which to think it—new tools indeed to *prompt us* to think it.

We are thus led further upstream, or *deeper underneath*, into the question of thought. As we might suspect, however, that "with which" I think (the point from which I begin to think)—beneath even that "about which" I think—is something I have trouble thinking, something I can approach only by *detour*[5]: not methodically (in the Cartesian manner) but by "cunning." I can reach it only by deviation, by *pulling free of the mire*. "Doubt" falls short (for do we even know what we are supposed to be doubting?). I must take an *oblique* approach, make use of a *divide*, and employ a *strategy*, because this is what gives me the means to think in the first place. Probing the notion of landscape, then, leads us back to what has organized the *work*[6] of thought in Europe. We are tempted to take these things for simple logical tools, all of them purportedly self-evident, but if we manage to step back to observe our landscape-thought, if we examine its historicity and fundamental choices, we might glimpse the singularity and *invention* with which those tools were forged. And our landscape-thought will in

---

5. The special term *detour* (*détour*) denotes the stepping into another culture's biases in order to avoid biases of our own culture, to reach the headwaters of our thought. [Translator's note.]

6. The special term *work* (*travail*) relates to Jullien's notion of the *chantier* (the active, conceptual dry dock where some activity takes place). Work continues so long as soaring continues. When work stops, when soaring falls into slackness, living comes to an end. [Translator's note.]

turn be clarified, once we have accounted for the condition of possibility that led to its advent.

Now that we have aroused our suspicions we quickly discern in European landscape-thought at least three substantial biases, whose incidence on the conception we must now gauge. They are of course known—all too "well known." But have we *probed* them? Has their all-too-well-knownness not in itself hindered their exploration? Right away we run into the fact, the discreet fact, that in Europe landscape was conceived in the shadow of the *part-whole* relation. A landscape, they tell us, is a "portion" of the land (land/landscape) that the observer's eye cuts out. Hence the delimiting "horizon." Yet I cannot help wondering what this odd thing called a "part" actually is. How deeply is our landscape-thought marked (affected) by dependence on a "whole"? The whole exceeds the *limited* part, which for this very reason becomes the landscape. We know this blind, as a matter of principle. But doesn't this shroud, reduce, and curtail the whole from the outset?

According to a second bias—readily (innocently) assumed to be self-evident, to need no further examination—landscape in Europe has been ascribed from the start, without the slightest discernible reluctance, to the primacy of *visual perception*. Our "piece of land" (says the *Robert* dictionary) is the part that nature "presents to an observer." In the usual definition the landscape "appears to the eye," or depends on a "vantage point." Here again, though, I wonder whether we shouldn't poke at the self-evidence of the *visual*, break up the monopoly (source of the obviousness), and achieve landscape's liberation. After all, isn't it "through" vision (or else what does "through" mean here?), by means of our eye and its domination, and by visual prospection alone, that we "accede" to landscape—that we tap its "resource"?

Finally, we cannot ignore another early structural influence on landscape-thought in Renaissance Europe. In parallel with the rise of science and its new apparatus, there was the ever so powerful *subject-object* relation. Indeed, it came first. It was the original bias. In the definition of science, the "observer" is on one side and "nature" on the other. The two are separate, established in a vis-à-vis.[7] In other words, our landscape-thought ended up "folded" into (along) the subject-object coupling that undergirds the knowledge from which modern Europe draws its strength. And hasn't it struggled ever since to escape that *fold*? Everything has been said on this score, and curses have rained down on the infernal coupling, but could we imagine never referring to it again? Criticize, renounce, and stigmatize it as we might, we depend on it still. Can our landscape-thought ever hope to *erase* it?

---

7. That is, they face each other across a divide (*écart*). [Translator's note.]

3

European landscape-thought has found its perch upon a sort of theoretical tripod, and I wonder whether the tripod hasn't furtively constrained our landscape-thought from the start. In particular, I wonder whether the first leg, the first perspective, hasn't exacted an automatic cost—an ontological loss, say—by letting us regard landscape in the contradictory light of the *part*. One might object that the "part" of the "land" that constitutes landscape is what detaches it from the "whole," brings it forth, and promotes it. As a fragment, though, doesn't the part remain dependent on the whole of the land that includes it—the whole of which it will always be a "portion"? For a "part," as the Greeks quickly realized, is in truth an odd thing. It is one *but* a part. It is indeed "one," because we isolate it and consider it separately. And because it is one it also constitutes a "whole." At the same time, however, it is not "one," because it is also a "part": because it belongs to a whole that, by integrating it, exceeds it.

Let us first pause to consider that our landscape-thought runs up against a paradox, one that the Greeks delighted in playing with (it so agreed with their penchant for exacting logic). A part is one because it exhibits a circumscription of its own. That is why we speak of "a" part. But a part is "not one" insofar as it is not completely isolated and insofar as it connects with other, neighboring parts. Otherwise it would not be a "part" (e.g., the hand's relation to the body in Galen). In landscape too the unity (the totality) is relative, contingent as it is on a mobile subject and thus on the perspectival shift that results with his every step, from his slightest displacement. As a mere part it bears a flaw deep within its being. It invokes a lack, or at any rate betrays its own limit—the limit delineated by the horizon, *horismos*, which, as the landscape's "definition," cuts the landscape out of space.

The notion of a "part" by itself thus entails something further. It casts yet another shadow on the "being" of landscape. Because it is considered a "portion of the land," landscape is understood with respect to the "expanse" of which it is a part—"expanse of land seen from a single angle," says the *Littré* dictionary. From the start, that is, we perceive landscape only with respect to what remains once we have subtracted bodily forms and have thus arrived at what is peculiar to the *expanse*. We perceive it only when there remains no differentiating property (as with the *res extensa* in Descartes). Better yet, let us say that once the abstraction is done the only property remaining to the expanse that makes up the excised land is homogeneity. This residual property of the *physical*, a matter of pure mathematics (i.e., yielding in principle to measurement and division), prompts us to forget the incommensurability, and thus the capacity for *individuation*, that is peculiar to landscape. Homogeneity buries the capacity for singularization beneath "isotropy," whereas it is precisely singularization that promotes landscape.

Moreover, "landscape" doubtless saw the light of day in European painting not merely because it was bounded by a horizon line, as if by a frame, but precisely because, as an expanse, it acceded to this geometric, uniform, and continuous space: because it both broke free of its former symbolic meanings and could at leisure be broken down into segments to meet the demands of perspectival projection. And if it came about this way, *via* the means and laws of representation alone, why should landscape not bear the mark of a preliminary stripping away of the sensible, and the subsequent neutralization of the "expanse" of which it is a "part"? Clearly, it needed but one more step—one further stage (the early twentieth century)—to arrive at an even more complete abstraction of space. But in taking that step we would also "go beyond" landscape and abandon it.

4

The second bias in the European definition of landscape is the *visual* bias, and it will seem equally impossible to dislodge. How can we expect even to *rattle* it, let alone get rid of it? At the same time, if a landscape is the portion of the land "that nature presents to the eye of the beholder," then isn't landscape doomed from the start to be passive? If it is something merely to "look at," then a landscape is subservient from the start to the initiative of the observer, who, as agent, sets the point of view. But do we in truth, *in effect*, only "look at" a landscape? (Or what, then, does "look at" mean?) Behind the pervasive, Western prejudice that, in our relationship to the world, grants primacy to visual perception lies the Greek choice—established at first blush, with no possible discussion and no hint of doubt—that vision is the superior sense. And when the eye can see no further the "eye of the soul" (*omma tēs psukhēs*, ὄμμα τῆς ψυχῆς) takes charge. The intelligible too is "visible" (in the mind). On this point the beginning of Aristotle's *Metaphysics* is categorical: vision prevails among our senses because it expands the range of difference, at least in the most discernable way, and by doing the work of distinction it already sets us on the path to knowledge.

With primacy granted to the visual, however, landscape was correlatively reduced to the *aspectual*. "Aspect" (*species*) denotes appearance to the eye and thus the characteristics and specificities of the outward. Thus by thinking of it in visual/aspectual terms we keep landscape on the surface, drain it of "traits," and keep ourselves on the outside. The resource runs dry already. By acceding to landscape through vision alone, moreover, we steer once more toward abstraction. The other senses (hearing and taste) are ambient, whereas vision *takes us out of the ambient*. It not only puts us at a remove but also *assigns*, and in so doing serves as the path to ontology. In other words, it fixes each object of perception in its proper place, in its "in itself" (*kath 'hauto*, in Greek), and there distinguishes and determines it. Vision thus leads us down the road to "essence." It leads us to the question "What is it?" or to "quiddity." It also costs us what I call *imbuing*.[8] But isn't *imbuing*—the "ambient" dimension—the prime (the most primordial) "promoter" of landscape?

5

If we wish to think of landscape as a *resource*, we must tarry no more and pry into the very things we consider "obvious." For more than a century European thought has been striving to renounce the separation of "subject" and "object," but however violently it has repudiated the separation, whatever titanic struggle it has endured to reverse the cleavage that it has so deftly—so conveniently—achieved, we must acknowledge (phenomenologically) that our landscape-thought issues from the very cleft, the very cradle, of that dissociation. It was born of the bipartition, even if it later oscillated between the resulting poles. To rethink landscape, then, we must grapple with an undeniable fact. Landscape-thought emerged, during the Renaissance, from a mytho(theo)logical notion of the universe. It emerged, that is, once the inherited symbolism of places was stripped away. But this emergence, as we all know (although *how far* have we taken this knowledge?), paralleled the invention of *objectivity*, which science then promoted (was promoted by).

Can our landscape-thought banish the cult of objectivization, the very thing to which we owe our creation of "nature"? The "object," fruit of long maturation during the Middle Ages, crosses Aristotle's opposite-correlated status (*antikeimenon*) with the notion of the *objectum*: what is "cast in front of" and blocks vision (according to the visual theory inherited from Augustine). It is one of Europe's "modern" inventions and its great tool. The object not only introduced a separation, airtight in principle, between man and the world but also gave to each a separate status, cleansing each of the other. Thus man became a subject with initiative,

---

8. The special term *imbuing* (*prégnance*) relates to ambience because it involves nothing that one could point at. What is imbued suffuses what it imbues. It is everywhere and nowhere. In this sense it stands opposed to the ontological, the determinate, and the assigned or assignable. In like manner, landscape, Jullien argues, is to be found nowhere in particular. What matters is not the place where we encounter landscape but the exploratory *divide* that opens between us and the land, prompting landscape's advent. [Translator's note.]

dependent only on himself (i.e., an autonomous subject), and the world became a knowable thing at which the mind could take aim "objectively," *intus objective*, because it was now free of incidental contamination. We know this "well," so well that we have grown tired of it. But have we taken full stock of the consequences?

It is momentous that landscape should be coeval with a world established not only in opposition to man but also in isolation from him: a world no longer colored by spiritual or merely affectual projections. This is so momentous, in fact, that there is now no escaping it. Our language itself has bowed (*folded*) before this reality. It can express nothing except in terms of the "choice," or the catenation, even when the choice itself is the very thing we hope to criticize. We can rebel against this state of affairs—this forcing of our hand—as much as we like; we can still never undo what has been done. We cannot prevent Europe's *invention of the "object."* There is no unfolding of that *fold*. We cannot undo the face-to-face where each is considered from the outset as separate from the other, and one as "before" the other. "Nature" stands always to one side, "presenting" the landscape as an "ob-ject," and the "observer" stands always to the other, positing himself as a "subject" at liberty. In Europe "landscape" will always presume the *exteriority of the spectator*. This is why the promotion of landscape has gone hand in hand with the geometric division of space: that is, with the transformation of space into a homogenous, isotropic, and infinite expanse, free of both topographical boundaries and symbolic assignations, and obeying the laws of optics alone. The subject has withdrawn to a "point of view," whose counterpart in the world is the "vanishing point."

Time and again Europe has reexamined the forcible geometric division of space, complained of the breach between interior and exterior, emotion and aspect, but this has changed nothing. At best it has only given a voice to frustrations pent up in a great theoretical edifice. Landscape has even served as the (Romantic) venue for the protest. "One does not make a landscape out of geometry," says Victor Hugo.[9] "If such-and-such assemblage of trees, mountains, waters, and houses, which we call a landscape, is beautiful, it is not through its own devices but through me," says Baudelaire, "through my own grace, through the idea or sentiment that attaches to it."[10] But suppose we *subsequently* repatriated landscape to the subjective side, returned it to the sphere of the intimate, and brought it back under the sway of sensibility or imagination. Would we thereby

---

9. "On ne fait pas un paysage avec de la géométrie." [Translator's note.]
10. "Si tel assemblage d'arbres, de montagnes, d'eaux et de maisons, que nous appelons paysage, est beau, ce n'est pas par lui-même, mais par moi, par ma grâce propre, par l'idée ou le sentiment qui s'y attache." [Translator's note.]

liberate it? Would we erase the stamp of dissociation, of what gave rise to it in the first place?

Returning landscape to the subject side might free it of the object's authority, but it would not deliver landscape from its quarrel with the object. It would not prevent landscape from oscillating between the two terms or indeed from conveying an exchange between them. We could restrict landscape to the projection of sentiment, making it into a vehicle for expression, or we could pretend to attain the truth of representation through landscape, as we have done in the past. Either way, however, we would come up short. We would henceforth be better off with more immediacy of sensation (less perceptual artifice), by remaining closer to "things," or else with a more deliberate, "conceptual," and outright inventive construction of the mind. And landscape would, again, remain in transition between the two, meeting the demands of neither. It was precisely by expunging landscape that twentieth-century art declared its refusal to perpetuate the to-and-fro.

6

In terms of the "object" relation, at any rate, we have already advanced far enough to distinguish between *landscape* and, say, "view." I suggest we ask a further question. When I look at Notre Dame de Paris from the Pont de l'Archevêché, or even from the next bridge, is there a "landscape"? I think not. There is a *view*, because there is a "view of" ("View of Notre Dame de Paris"). There is a view because there is a *possible object*. "Ob"–"ject," from "cast" "in front of." It obstructs my vision and takes precedence in my attention. I cannot help but look at it. My vision is stirred, its scrutinizing faculties engaged, with respect to the object. All else lies around it, borders it, and serves as mere decor. There is a "view" because there is a focus. My eye engages, fixes the object in admiration. It discerns and catalogs ever more perfection in it. *For there to be landscape*, however, there must be nothing left to impose its hegemony; there must be nothing to hold the eye. This is why *variety* figures as one of the chief predicates in the list of landscape's criteria. *Variety* is not anecdotal, like *bucolic*, and is thus perhaps landscape's most suitable qualifier.

There is thus no landscape unless there is a de-concentration, or unfixing, of the eye. The eye must circulate. It must wander for a landscape to arise. And indeed, from the Pont de Sully, one bridge farther off, things begin to change. There is now no longer a "view of." A landscape begins to take shape. There is now no object to draw the eye's focus (no monument). Elements, or constituent vectors, emerge and face off, responding to one another. We have the horizontality of water in motion and the fixed verticality of the towers, the lush clumps of trees along the riverbanks, and the drily rectilinear traffic lanes. Distance is not the sole contributor, but with the remove contrary factors come into correlation, spread out, and cooperate on equal terms, urging the eye toward a conversion: inviting the eye no longer to come to rest "on" anything but to come and go from one thing to another—or rather *between* them.

If I speak of a "View of the Seine" (in painting), it can be only a "view of the Seine at . . . ." A "view of" inevitably creates the effect of an assignation. But a landscape of the "banks of the Seine" makes any assignation *evasive*. Two things prevail: a divide in the very heart of the visible, which sets the visible in tension, and a subsequent, indefinite play of interactions between the constituent elements. Thus the reference distends (the object crumbles) and a landscape (in painting) cannot *resemble*. For there to be "landscape" the monopoly that generates visual adhesion-fixation must blur and polarities must come into play that entice the eye to circulate. In other words, opposition and correlation must deploy concurrently, *between* factors. This then gives the eye leave to disengage from its visual obsessions and *roam*. And thus the eye, now serving a new purpose, can devote itself to opening wide and taking in, allowing passage and exchange.

A view is "beautiful." Notre Dame de Paris seen from the Pont de l'Archevêché is beautiful (indeed, do I know of anything more beautiful?). Beautiful, "more beautiful than," in terms of the "view" (of the object): even the comparative is justified. But I am not certain that a landscape can "be beautiful," even if *beautiful* is the predicate most often appended to it in our European languages. I am not sure that *beautiful* is altogether pertinent when applied "to" a landscape, that it is not simply a facile way to settle our accounts with landscape (we would at least have to follow Baudelaire and say "sad and beautiful . . ."). *Beautiful* claps itself visually (aspectually) to the surface and thus reduces the resource harbored by the landscape. We say "beautiful" before a landscape (is it pertinent even to say "before"?) because we know of nothing else to say, because of the conventions or laziness of language, or because we are labeling the landscape. We do this, in sum, to spare ourselves from having to confront, from having to seek out within ourselves (even as we remark "ourselves"), what the landscape has suddenly caused to arise. The "world's most beautiful landscape," says Voltaire, finding a convenient, superlative (abstract), and despicable way to shunt it aside.

Can we yet "describe" a landscape? The question is all the more apt insofar as there is no proper "object" under consideration or resemblance to seek out. We can describe a "view of." For instance, I do not care for the first lines of *The Red and the Black*, the description of Verrières. It smacks of guidebooks and their "views of." (Of course, Stendhal did write in the tourist genre to earn his keep.) It would seem that Stendhal knew no better than to catalog the picturesque in purely additive, well-crafted (well-written) prose. Characterizing and complaisantly laudatory, it sets up no tensions, allows nothing to resonate. Stendhal ought to have helped us penetrate into the little town's activity and society. If we are to *enter*, then M. de Rênal must appear as the provincial man of influence, at the summit of his glory and already under threat. There must be tension set up (Stendhal's lines would need to find a way to *deploy*). If in fact only objects are open to description, shall we say that landscapes are "evoked"? Well, to evoke is to invite into partnership, as we might evoke a loved one, or an absent friend. We would conjure his presence once more, like something we already feared to part with. We would confer the power to arouse in us at length, dreamily, nostalgically . . . we know not what (for we now lack an "object"). We are done with "characteristics" and aspectual traits. We lose ourselves, rapt, in the landscape.

7

Though we separate "view" from landscape—"describing" the one / "evoking" the other—we will struggle to dismiss the misgivings of common sense. It is not merely because we are clinging to some ancient Greek predilection for visual perception that we conceive of landscape in terms of vision. Nor is it because landscape is what nature "presents to an observer," as the aforementioned definition says. There is another, obvious reason: we accede to landscape by looking. Indeed, the *Robert* dictionary's first illustrative example of the verb *look* is "to look at the landscape." Perhaps we should take a step further, or a step back, and ask what exactly we mean by "looking." Is *look* truly a simple, unitary verb limited to the function described, or is the verb itself perhaps distended between two possibilities? To "accede" to landscape we must, I believe, discern the one beneath the other.

Once again, this amounts to asking whether I can look at a landscape the way I look at an "ob-ject," at a church or forest standing before me, or even at a far-off airplane crossing the sky. Or whether the act of looking splits in two, insofar as I either "observe" (the verb traditionally associated with "landscape") or *become receptive*. Either my gaze ventures "in front of" (the *ob* of ob-stacle and ob-ject) or I *allow it to spill over*. Either my gaze projects outward, seeking external information, scrutinizing, questing, as if on the hunt (the object becoming the objective), or else I receive through (into) my eye what pours in from the world, what my eye allows to pass through it—to the point where I let the world-pouring-in permeate me and drown my attention. The disengagement of *allow* (*lassen*): In looking I now gather in a diffuse way, just as I gather with my ear when I hear. Is *observe*, then, really the apt word when it comes to landscape? We employ it readily enough (the "observer" before nature), but really it denotes deliberate, voluntary attention—attention trained (once again) on the quest for knowledge. In truth, there is something militaristic and vigilant about the word. And indeed, as Yves Lacoste has remarked, in Europe the "aesthetic" perception of landscape has continually run parallel to tactical observation: the same privilege is accorded, notably, to the "vantage point."

Certain things leave us tongue-tied when we try to say them in European language. For this Plato himself—albeit incidentally—can come to our aid. A distinction he makes in passing in the *Theaetetus* (184 b–d) offers a thread for us to follow as we steer "look" out of its fake unity. Positing two cases in language, Plato asks whether we see "with our eyes" (dative case in the Greek) or "through our eyes" (*dia* + genitive). In the first instance our eyes are agents (autonomous, possessing active power). In the second they are mere instruments and thus, says Plato, serve an authority within us. This authority, "whether we should call it soul or something else," makes use of the eyes. Plato seizes on the second case exclusively. He attributes agency systematically to the soul, relegating the eyes, and the senses generally, to the subservient role of instrument. I wonder, though, whether we might instead use the two parallel structures to distinguish *two possible cases*. In other words, we might instead posit two different ways of looking.

Rather than dwell on these linguistic subtleties (Plato himself scorns such minutiae), I would like to open a preliminary divide and restore some latitude to "looking." On the one hand, I can look "with my eyes," in which case my eyes are agents. I "observe" and seek to determine what things are and to describe "objects" by sight. On the other, I can look "through my eyes," in which case my eyes are the way or the means, the threshold or the window. I no longer look "at something"; I simply look. My gaze is attentive while it also *becomes evasive*. My attention, we might say, is "floating," or available. I no longer "observe." Instead, as language does its best to say, I "contemplate." *Contemplate*, from the Latin, at the least casts a broader spectrum. We need only recall that contemplation harks back to the square space (the *templum*) that an augur would delimit in the sky and on the earth. Within this space he would gather and interpret signs. The eye *allows* things—*all* things that are able—to pass into the visual field, assemble, and enter into relationships. Thus we can understand that in allowing this the gaze lends itself to the meditative, to dreaminess. The eyes, then, are not so much agents as intermediaries: vectors or ferrymen providing passage so that landscape can penetrate deep within us.

This is the first definition of landscape (of what "gives rise to landscape") that I propose as a corrective to the aforementioned ordinary definition. There is "landscape" when this conversion of the eye takes place. This is not the conversion belabored by metaphysics, where, as desire awakens, the eye is turned away from the things of this world and toward things that are Out There and in the "realm of ideas" (Plato). Nor, to phrase it differently, is it a conversion that turns the eye from the world's outside to the soul's "inside" (the *endon* in Plotinus). The operative *conversion of the eye* here assumes no break or forsaking. But there is landscape when the common type of perception, reconnaissance, and observation, in which the eyes are agents, allows itself to be overwhelmed by the other type, in which the eye no longer seeks for identification or information but instead allows itself to be "absorbed." Let us adopt this term for the moment. The gaze does not cast itself into the world and retrieve, like so much netted game, as much of the object as the subject needs to get its bearings. Instead the gaze gives us occasion to pry into the relations of things, to immerse ourselves in the tension-setting network of oppositions-correlations. "Subject-hood" is thereby undone simultaneously (proportionately) as initiative and as monopoly. Moreover, we can now gaze for more than an instant, or more than whatever time we need to complete an observation. Truth be told, the eye thus used has no reason to stop "roaming," from one thing to another—or rather *between* them—as it is bandied about by their polarities and loses itself in their profusion.

II

"Mountain(s)-Water(s)"

1

China presents us with a whole other approach to what we in Europe call "landscape." It breaks radically with the semantics of the expanse, the view, and the cutoff. It offers us "mountain(s)-water(s)," *shan shui* (山水), or "mountain(s)-river(s)," *shan chuan* (山川). The term dates to antiquity but is just as current now, in modern Chinese, as it was then. It has been neither replaced nor altered, even through contact with European influence, and has suffered no wear. Its fundamental bias endures; its semantic choice still goes unquestioned. The Chinese have wondered over it no more than we in Europe have wondered over the foundations of "landscape." And yet in China we are thinking no longer of a portion of the land offered up to an observer's eye but of a correlation of opposites: "mountains" and "waters."

"Mountain(s)"/"water(s)." We have what tends toward heights (the mountain) and what tends toward depths (the water). The vertical and the horizontal, High and Low, at once oppose and respond to each other. We have, too, what is immobile and impassive (the mountain) and what is in constant motion, forever undulant and flowing (the water). Permanence and variance are at the same time confronted and associated. We have, moreover, what possesses form and presents a relief (the mountain) and what is by nature formless and takes the form of other things (the water). The opaque and the transparent, the solid and the dispersive, and the stable and the fluid blend together and heighten each other. We have, finally, what lies frontally before our eyes, and we look at (the mountain) and what we hear from various sides and whose rustle reaches our ears (the water). Our sight and our hearing too are called into play.

Instantly we get a powerful break with the semantics of territory ("land"/"landscape"), of the specifying part, and of exclusive reliance on vision. Instead of the unitary term *landscape*, China speaks of an endless play of interactions between contrary factors that pair up, forming a matrix through which the world is conceived and organized. Here there is no governing, dominating Subject (the Renaissance subject of Europe), no individual to hold the world from his vantage point and to develop his initiative freely within it, as if he were God. There is no "ob"–"ject" held in vis-à-vis, nothing to be "cast" "before" the individual's eye, nothing to spread out passively for his inspection and cut itself out differently with his every step. Against this monopolizing power of sight China offers the essential polarity through which *world-stuff* enters into tension and deploys. No *human-stuff* detaches from this. The human remains implicit, contained within these multiple implications, because the vis-à-vis thus established lies within the world; it is *between* the "mountains" and the "waters."

It falls to landscape—"mountain(s)"/"water(s)"—to gather, condense, and raise into the realm of sensibility what opens up between the poles. (This is *polarity* exactly as it applies to the physical or the organic.) The world proceeds from what opens between the poles: between High and Low, the immobile and the undulant, the opaque and the transparent, the solid and the fluid, and indeed the seen and the heard. Rather than envisage landscape from the perspective of what we once called *species*, or from any of the term's various meanings—the power of sight, aspect, and specification—China's opposing-correlating "mountain(s)"/"water(s)" instantly plunges us into the network of factors that give rise to the "world"—through which "there is world"—and that keep it *soaring* [*en essor*].[1] We find ourselves *immersed* in it. There is no "nature" that "presents to the eye," for nature is nothing but the continual interaction between the aforementioned poles and will not be instantiated as a separate agent. Nor is there an "observer" to face the landscape, no one to remain outside and delimit the horizon by virtue of his position. The vantage point of no subject casts its partiality over the cooperation of factors concentrated in landscape.

What advantage, I ask, might China's approach to what we call "landscape" provide us over the traditional European approach? The European tradition has only gone in circles, returning time and again to the obstinate semantics of "land"/"landscape." Has it perhaps been spinning its

---

1. In Jullien's special lexicon, soaring (*l'essor*) is the opposite of slackness (*l'étale*). What soars is alive, partakes in *living*, and remains processual, whereas what slackens dies, comes to an end, and becomes definite. [Translator's note.]

wheels in a mire from which it has perhaps never come unstuck? In this respect there is indeed a European "tradition," regardless of reservations we might now have about the term. And we can gauge this tradition only from the outside, regardless of Europe's efforts to get out of its rut, self-criticize, and effect a renewal; regardless of its claims to have made a clean break, wipe its concept clean, and think of landscape in a new, "modern" way. We have remained beholden to the semantics of land/landscape and to all that they imply. The semantics are sediment now. They amount to a choice that we do not realize has been made.

In looking elsewhere, however, we find a chance to start fresh. We are given a new, unexpected way to think about what we in Europe continue to call "landscape." Suddenly we need no longer be the prisoners of a jailer whose very existence we have never suspected. We were not expecting this other possibility of thought. In truth, we *had never even imagined it*. It offers itself up to our minds, never forcing its way, never even ruffling any feathers. It is not so very "strange" and gradually insinuates itself. It is already "speaking" to us, though it cost us a complete reconfiguration, an as-yet-implicit reconfiguration, of our categories. We cannot yet tell how far it will go. It gives us a grip, something to hold on to, an *angle* (an angle of approach, as they say). The term is operative, for my purpose in using Chinese thought is to exploit such new and un-dreamed-of angles. At last we will stop allowing the mind to glide along on the all-too-slippery walls of our familiar representations. We will once more find a foothold—indeed, a ledge to support us and allow us to advance.

The time has come to ask whether we have had the right tools to engage in the thought of what we call "landscape." What might we have overlooked, through carelessness, or through use of our mistaken tools? Might our tools have somehow "crippled" us? Suppose we choose, as I have chosen, to contemplate the coherences that have developed in various cultures while yet not losing sight of the divide between said cultures. Suppose we regard these coherences as so many potential resources with which to think through *the common*[2] in our experience. In the Chinese approach to what (for lack of another name) we call "landscape," in the "mountains" and "waters" that this approach presents us with, might there not be a dormant fecundity, one that perhaps we need only stir from the atavism where Chinese tradition—itself subject to "self-evidence"—has plunged it and let it languish? Could this in turn stir *us* from *our own* atavism?

---

2. The common (*le commun*), for Jullien, comes to light once cultures that are set face-to-face across a *divide* have reflected each other, each bringing to light what lies beneath the other's biases. [Translator's note.]

2

What, in fact, has happened in the passage from "landscape" to "mountain(s)-water(s)," and from one language to the other, each in ignorance of the other? We have in one fell swoop left behind the question of the "expanse," with its abstraction of appreciable qualities (its reductive focus on spatial dimension alone), and entered a field of countless tensions, and as many cooperating oppositions. Now, with every "vantage point" withdrawn, there is no longer a world spread before me, detaching from the self-subject as a view or a spectacle, at once blocking the extension of my gaze and, by halting it, bringing it into focus. No longer "before," I am now *between*. Now "I" am integrated. "What lies between Heaven and Earth [天地之间]," says Laozi, "is it not like a great bellows?" (§7). The insufflation generated in the "interspace" tirelessly imbues with life. Landscape—"mountain(s)/water(s)"—is the appreciable investment of this life. It immerses us instantly in the play of manifestations of energy, manifestations that both conflict and pair up. All *vitality* (we might as well call it reality) is there revealed.

Moreover, whereas "landscape" can be individualized and thus spoken of in the singular, or in units ("a" landscape), "mountain(s)-water(s)" functions as a pair. It folds in on its inner relation alone, closes itself off in its correlation, and thus speaks to a tension that is common to *all* landscape. Furthermore, landscape as conceived in China is never local (as in "a part of the land") but is understood globally. It proceeds through *pairing*, with a logic that nothing escapes and that "mountains" and "waters" totalize. In China, then, a landscape is never a "corner" of the world. It is always—within its very configuration, its singular configuration—the result or, better yet, the *operation of the world* in its entirety. Even as it individualizes it is, let us say, "cosmic." Thus we escape the ambiguity of the "part": the part that is at once one and not-one, the part that is only a part but is as such also a whole. "Landscape arises," Chinese tells us, when it forgets that it is a part and imposes itself instantly as a whole and when we find everything (all manner of things) in it, because everything in it is contrasted and conjoined. There is landscape when I find in it both the one and the other: the stable and the fluid, the vertical and the horizontal, the solid and the dispersive, or the seen and the heard.

At this point there arises a divide that leads us further upstream, and on either side of the divide we conduct a broader, more patient exploration of the logic behind the biases that have produced our two disparate conceptions of landscape. Following these two trails we will better understand how our landscape-thought was shaped by *choices* that it did not probe, choices that it never imagined were even available. Why should Europe have detached *landscape* from *land*? And why should it previously have cut landscape into a "part" only to promote it simultaneously as a "whole"? By thinking in terms of the paradox where a part is also a whole, European thought has from the start, I believe, situated landscape within the logic of *composition*, which ever since the Greeks has structured European reason with regard to things.

The logic of composition exists at every level. *All the levels align.* Whether we speak of the fundamental elements in physics, the parts of the body in medicine, or the constitution in politics (citizens, says Aristotle, are "parts" of the whole that is the polis), the principle is always the same. We organize the field to be explored by detaching and separating it from a whole (showing the singular unit to be a whole) and, to reverse the procedure, by attaching it to and integrating it with the whole (showing the whole to be a mere part). The two procedures go hand in hand. It is through *com-position* that we in Europe com-prehend. But the *organon* is not self-evident. We have thought it universal because compositional logic is embedded in our language. Its fundamental schema, as the Greeks themselves observed, is the structure of the alphabet (letters, as units, come to compose syllables, words, phrases, and speech), and it has ruled over all knowledge. It has ruled over geometry (from point to line, surface, and volume) as well as anatomy (each part of the body, broken down as far as it will go, revealing its function at ever larger scales in the whole). Such was the method of the mind itself, from Plato to Descartes. "Analysis" divides into constituent parts, and "synthesis" reassembles from these a coherent whole.

3

In China the correlation of "mountains" and "waters" presents us with a different choice of the mind, a choice whose logic proceeds not from composition but from what I have begun to call *pairing*. Here "the one" is never without "the other." They are hitched together. Each is the other's reply. In China to think is to "couple," as the language itself demonstrates. Chinese writing is ideographic and has never known alphabetic composition. In its brush strokes it alternates and correlates the "void" and the "full," the "high" and the "low," the "thick" and the "thin," the "dense" and the "sparse," or what "tends toward" and what "turns its back" (*xiang bei*, 向背). Moreover, the Chinese language knows nothing of syntax, with the attendant hierarchies and subordinating agreements. Through parataxis, however, it favors "parallels" (although even this term is too aspectual). Statements are made with respect to symmetrical others in opposition-coupling, as we see even in the earliest divinatory inscriptions, on bones and carapaces. As "Heaven" responds to "Earth," "mountain" responds to "water."

Nowhere in all the knowledge of China would we find anything but this same convention. Chinese thought has molded itself so thoroughly on *coherence by coupling* that sinologists are no longer surprised. They no longer even see it. What field of knowledge, what sector of activity, falls outside its scope? Chinese physics developed on the basis not of fundamental elements or atoms (the *stoicheia*, στοιχεία, of the Greeks) but of "agents" or vectors (*wu xing*, 五行) entering into oppositions-correlations that follow upon one another in alternation. Magnetism may have lingered in its infancy in Europe, but in China it developed early, precisely because the Chinese were so attentive to the phenomena of polarity and attraction. Chinese medicine, meanwhile, neglected anatomical knowledge and instead thought of our physical being as a whole of correlative factors. This whole was explored by the acupuncturist, each point of energy having its responsive counterpart. For this same reason China showed hardly any interest in constructing geometric figures and focused instead on algebra and algorithmic transformations. The philosophy of power, moreover, was in China never based on the composition of a body politic (no *demos*) but conceived as a correlation between the prince and the people (between father and son), each promoting its virtue with respect to the other in pure reciprocity. We need only recall that *dui* (对), which even in contemporary Chinese signifies "just/apt," or "exact," designates the "couple" or the "pair." It signifies that the one forms a couple with the other; the one finds a partner, and thus also its "justification," in the other.

Time and again I turn to a particular example, because I find it so very eloquent. To say "thing" in Chinese, even in modern Chinese (it is one of the first words taught), you utter not a unitary term, not "thing" (*causa*), not a thing you attend to, or "make your business" (and not *res*, substance, either), but "east-west," *dong xi* (东西). This term—this couple, rather—exemplifies the essential correlation through which China approaches landscape: "mountain(s)-water(s)." I sometimes hear the retort that this is just "a manner of speaking," but a manner of speaking is always, indissociably, a *manner of thinking*. We can easily see that "thing," though the most (seemingly) neutral and indeterminate of terms, is already slicing and dicing. It is already focusing, already pointing at the elementary and the substantial (and why not at sexual fixation, as in the French phrase *"être porté sur la chose,"* that is, "be obsessed with sex"?). With "east-west," meanwhile, we approach everything in terms of polarity. What is primary, what denotes, is the fact of the *relation*. Partners emerge in a vis-à-vis. They form an "east-west." A tension is set up. An engendering of "world-stuff" begins. And "mountain(s)/water(s)" is the "landscaped" manifestation.

Yin/yang penetrates so straight to the heart of the exceedingly general logic of pairing that we no longer translate it. From the apex down, a mountain's two sides diverge, one remaining in shadow while the other is lit by the rising sun (*adret* and *ubac*, in the primary sense of the terms[3]), but each remains indissociable from—and indeed inconceivable without—the other. The same goes for heaven and earth, the "hard" and the "soft," the "initiator" and the "receiver" (the first two figures of the *Classic of Changes*, or *I-Ching*), the masculine and the feminine, or the prince and the people. The one exists only in opposition to the other and only by virtue of its *inseparability* from the other. It "is" only in relation with the other. This is why Chinese language-thought does not say "being" in the absolute sense, in the sense of "existence," by isolating it (though only in its predicative use). It cannot properly say "I *am*," "*ego sum*," and thus does not conceive of an insular, let alone solipsistic, "I." It does not conceive of the very "I" that detaches itself in the "vantage point."

In the same way, the "mountain" is not thought of, does not exist, "in itself," apart and withdrawn in its essence. The "mountain" assumes—necessarily calls forth—its partner: the "water." Yin/yang speaks to the interaction of factors or "capacities" at work in all polarity (*de*, 德). "Heaven/earth" denotes the instantiated global framework. (Indeed, Chinese thought achieved its originality when, in Chinese antiquity, it plucked heaven from its isolation and coupled it with the earth.) "East-west" horizontally deploys the divide that sets up tension between "things" and brings about their *advent*. And, finally, "mountain(s)/water(s)" makes the polarity perceptible in its physicality. Here, however, it unfolds the polarity vertically, as if across the various, infinite, incessant play of its manifestations.

4

We might never suspect the wealth of notional choices contained in each of these conceptions—the Chinese and the European—by virtue of their semantics. We might never suspect it, that is, unless we set them side by side, so that they can reflect each other. In this we do not so much perform a "comparison," in the proper sense, as have each interrogate the other—and thus hoist both at last out of their respective tacit implications. Through this mutual face-off we can venture back into their unthought-of. Each is ensnared (imprisoned) in its coherence. Each is walled up—and sits mute—in what it sees as obvious; each finds comfort in its biases. In taking a step further we get proof of just how radical the divide is: to wit, the incidence of this divide, "landscape," can in Europe easily make

---

3. In other words, as Jullien writes, the respective sunny and shady sides of a mountain. [Translator's note.]

use of a figurative meaning to venture into abstraction. Thus we speak of a cultural, intellectual, or political landscape. "Your soul is a chosen landscape . . . ."[4] There is someone from the outside, an "observer," to consider the *aspectual* nature of the composition.

As we might imagine, though, "mountain(s)-water(s)" does not drift so easily into such abstraction. "Mountain(s)-water(s)" keeps us in the "being-there" (*da sein*) of polarized tension and the contrary capacities that pair off therein. Confucius was already drawing a parallel between the two terms. When he says that the "wise man" likes ("finds pleasure in") water and that the "good man" likes ("finds pleasure in") mountains (*Analects*, VI, 21) both water and mountains retain their strict sense even as they symbolize. There might be a preference for the one or the other, water or mountains, because of their respective attractions: that is, insofar as they are poles generating an affinity. The "wise man" likes *water* because his intelligence is supple and fluid, like water itself, whereas the "good man" likes *mountains* because he is firm and constant, like the mountains themselves. This, Confucius goes on to say, is why the wise man is drawn to "motion" and the good man to "calm." Alternatively, this is why the wise man tends toward joy (in the moment): water is endlessly renewing itself as it follows its course. The good man, meanwhile, tends toward longevity: the mountain, ever stable, is changeless.

5

When it saw the light of day in China, as early as the start of the fifth century, landscape poetry was conceived—and presented—as a simple connection of "mountains" and "water." It did not venture beyond the thought to which the pairing led. All it did was unfold the couple and take advantage of the resulting play of polarities. In the autumn of 422, headed for the post to which he had been dispatched, on the East China Sea, the poet Xie Lingyun took a side trip to his property in Shining and wrote a poem. What follows is a word-for-word translation,[5] to avoid stemming the flow of poetic invention and thereby betraying the effect of continual coupling:

Mountain(s)   cross   go the whole   climb   descend
                        way

---

4. The first line ("*Votre âme est un paysage choisi* . . .") of "*Clair de Lune*," a poem by Paul Verlaine. [Translator's note.]

5. The English is a word-for-word translation of Jullien's French translation. [Translator's note.]

Water(s)	reach	go through to the end	go upstream	rush down
Peaks	stand tall	summits	link up	rising in stages
Beaches	unfold	islets	tie together	appearing in succession

The verses are read two by two, in both transverse (vertical) and linear fashion, and the entire poem proceeds from a pairing in which each term receives and responds to a counterpart. The first term in the first verse ("mountains") is already *awaiting* its other, which arrives in the following verse ("waters"). Through this correspondence the one is reflected in the other and *is heard through that other*. Its sole justification lies in the resulting tension, and from that tension derives its "aptness."

"Mountain(s)—cross . . ." / "Water(s)—reach . . . ." Because the Chinese language knows no declension or conjugation, calls on no preposition, adverb, or conjunction, and needs no circumstantial or modal marker, the correlating vis-à-vis from verse to verse is stark and raw. There is nothing to dilute or temper it. The utterance is not discursive. It is not continually inaugurating a "meaning" as the same phrase in European language inevitably must ("I stroll in the mountains, going all the way . . ."). But it is *co-herent* through and through. It takes opposites and "holds them together." (Here *meaning* and *coherence* are to be understood as opposites, not as synonyms.) Thus I would not render these first two verses in the manner of their most esteemed translator, J. D. Frodsham, who transforms them into a descriptive-narrative utterance and places them predicatively under the authority of a subject:

> Climbing and camping in mountains has quite worn me out,
> I'm weary of fording rivers, of pushing on downstream and up.[6]

A translation like this is not, properly speaking, false, but in drowning out the rigorous coupling it does destroy the poetic effect. The poetic effect is, quite simply, the *effect of realness*, and thus the translation also misses what in the poem gives rise to "landscape."

We observe, moreover, that nothing in the poem individualizes the position of a self-subject or is set up as a vantage point. What we call landscape is approached, from the two *coordinators* of mountains and waters, only *through activity*. We walk, stroll, and wander. We explore the landscape end to end, pace it out to the point of exhaustion. The mountain reveals its secrets as we make our way up or down (*deng/dun*), and

---

6. Xie Lingyun, "Guo Shining shu"; cf. J. D. Frodsham, *The Murmuring Stream* (Kuala Lumpur, Malaysia: University of Malaya Press, 1967), 1:118.

the water invites us to follow it up- and downstream (*hui/yan*). It is by ascending and descending that we enter into landscape. It is by traversing it end to end that we deploy it. There is no verb here to indicate any gazing, or else the function of gazing remains immersed. The landscape unfolds in the vertical-horizontal: in the mountain's rise / in the water's flow. The same succession of peaks and summits / of sand banks and islets opens unto depths as we make our way in. Folds (in the mountains) and meanderings (in the waters) stretch off into the distance. There is no horizon to delimit a territory, to cut it into a "part."

The following two verses develop strictly through variation of pairing:

| White | cloud(s) | enlace | remote | rock(s) |
| Green | bamboo(s) | attract | limpid | wave(s) |

"Rock(s)" and "wave(s)" simultaneously condense and localize—metonymize—the fundamental tension of mountain and water. The one's compact anchoring responds to the other's slight undulation. To apprehend what gives rise to landscape, then, we always refer to this reticulate play of correlations: in the one verse and the other, "remote" and "limpid" are—through their coupling, their emancipatory coupling—not so much descriptive (of qualities) as evocative of an *environment*. (They are freed both from court intrigues and from sullying society.) In like manner, "enlace" and "attract" speak conjointly to an envelopment in the resulting plenty and calm. A landscape (or landscape in general) deploys in the interspace that, by means of a divide, opens between manifestations and "capacities" that themselves activate and stoke each other in their opposition. To the ("white") clouds, blurring distant summits with their nimbus, respond the young (green) bamboos, nearby and distinct. This is less a landscape panorama spread before us (a "lovely panorama," as our guidebooks say) than a landscape that develops into a *milieu*—where, through multiple tensions, *living* soars anew, finds emancipations, and intensifies. By withdrawing into the realm of "mountains" and "waters" we have entered a denser network. Ramifications compound, energies echo, and potentialities align. In other words, pairings play out in full. The poetic economy of these few verses is enough to produce a "whole" of the world—indeed, a world that lacks for nothing.

6

The "gaze" goes unmentioned. If we like, though, we can infer it, *in fine*, from the following two verses, before the departing poet announces his plan to return. But even our inference passes through the conjunction of two dimensions: the sinuous waters / the succeeding mountains:

| Repair | house | leans out over | sinuousness | rivers |
| Erect | belvedere | lay basis for | succession | summits |

Once again, the idea is less to contemplate the landscape than to *anchor* ourselves in it and dwell there. Rather than consider the landscape from a single, privileged point (the ideal position of a dominant "subject"), from the point that an observer would momentarily occupy to contemplate what lies before him (the "vantage point") and enjoy the widest possible field of vision (the "beauty," we say, of a "panorama"), we instead establish *two* respective and reciprocal positions *within the landscape itself*. We do it enduringly (we build). These positions in turn oppose and respond to each other, and allow us to envisage the landscape, alternately, from the one or the other: from high to low or low to high, from an overlook onto the river or from a base at the foot of the mountains. *Between* them *immersion* takes place.

Look, moreover, is not a unitary verb in Chinese. It is neither neutral nor general. Rather, we utter it differently depending on our position and the manner of our looking. Our poet uses it in other poems like so many concurrent verbs, none prevailing over the others. He might just as easily say "(look) obliquely" (*lai*, 睐) as "(look) with a turn of the head" (*gu*, 顾), "(look) with an opposite turn of the head" (*juan*, 眷), "(look) in contemplation" (*lan*, 览), "(look) wide-eyed" (*tiao*, 眺), "(look) with absorption" (*du*, 睹), "(look) into the distance" (*yao wang*, 遥望), "(look) with a galloping eye" (*cheng wang*, 骋望), or yet "(look) from on high" (*kan*, 瞰), and so on. These are so many different ways of engaging with the world, ways that will not be subsumed under a single concept of vision. *Look* will not be generalized from an attitude, will not be limited to the act of looking. It is behavioral as well. There remains something both gestural and situational about it. In other words, looking will not be separated into a pure faculty of knowledge or enter into a neutral face-to-face with *things*, which under the tension of a divide, go by the name "east-west" (东西) in Chinese. From this "east-west" the poet extends the couple to the landscape, for a complete ("cosmic") pairing:[7]

Turn the gaze	west	one would say	rise	moon
卷	西	谓	初	月
Turn the gaze the other way	east	one wonders	set	sun
顾	东	疑	落	日

---

7. "Deng yongjia Lüzhang shan."

Look unmoors neither from its physical implications nor from the polarities that give rise to the world. In "turn the gaze to the west" / "turn the gaze to the east" we plunge into the clockwork of celestial motions, the rise and set of the heavenly bodies. All landscape apprehended in this play of correlations is the entirety of the world in its vibrancy: not a world that beckons from Elsewhere but a world perceived in the to-and-fro of its respiration. This same tension of *living* is what Chinese painting captures in landscape.

III

From a Landscape to Living

1

Here the comparativists will find something of interest. The notion of landscape arose in Europe in relation to painting. Well, China tells more or less the same tale, even if the pairing of "mountains and waters" goes back to antiquity. We observe, in any case, that Chinese painters adopted the term early on and then developed it. In both traditions, moreover, we observe the same transition, in which scenes and characters are set aside in favor of landscape. What are we to make of this common destiny? Might it be due to some need within painting itself? After all, the evolution took place on both sides and we have no reason to suspect any influence or contamination between worlds that knew nothing of each other. There is a divide, however, in the date of the change: a millennium earlier in China than in Europe. The reason, no doubt, is that China had been unrestrained by any of Europe's fetters. To put it positively, the Chinese pairing of "mountains and waters" in itself called forth this development in painting. In sum, the concepts of painting and landscape were in China compelled to agree.

Remember, landscape painting in Europe arose on the fringes of official painting: of commissioned, official painting. It arose, as it were, on the side. We see it in the plates of herbaria, in the carefully realistic illustrated environments of pharmacopeias and hygienic treatises, and in the seasonal, illuminated decor of the *Très riches heures du Duc de Berry*. We see it later, more openly, in European painting's background "window," with its framing of sinuous rivers and bluish mountains. Thus we get a sense of the European painter's patience—indeed, perseverance—in his strivings for landscape. When it finally emerges landscape is but a timid presence on the margins, because margins abide more improvisation and independence. There one could take greater liberties with respect to the imposed subject and technique. In this context naturalness in landscape is achieved, aptly enough, only at the cost of de-symbolizing and "secularizing" the world.[1] Thus it is only by compromise, only by accepting more or less felicitous solutions, that landscape gradually earns its place, gradually stakes its claim, beneath the domination of the scene and *historia*. We get either landscape backgrounds where foreground scenes increasingly struggle to fit in (Patinir) or small formats that are mere sidelights to the work, *parerga*, and deemed unworthy of attention (Dürer).

Chinese landscape stands in stark contrast with European landscape's terribly slow birth in painting. The development in China from character painting to landscape painting is the development of painting itself. It is concurrent with painting's embrace of its own vocation. It goes hand in hand with the emancipation from resemblance, a constraint, we observe, that Chinese painting sloughed off in successive molts, and with little apparent effort, famously considering it mere "child's play." In the retrospective, recapitulative judgment of Su Dongpo, the lettered, eleventh-century coiner of the phrase, two categories stand diametrically opposed and divide painting into two camps. The first of these, deemed definitively inferior, comes higgledy-piggledy and is, as it were, jettisoned. It is the painting "of men, of animals, of palaces, and of utensils" whose "constant form" (*chang xing*, 常形) is imposed on the painter.[2] One need only reproduce this form faithfully—"formally"—to meet the sole criterion of technique. The second category—this one homogeneous—is that of "mountains, rocks, bamboos, trees, waters, waves, vapors, clouds." As they have no "constant form," their *constancy* is of another order. It stems from the principle of *internal coherence* at the root of their advent (*chang li*, 常理). It falls to the painter to grasp and depict this, and he must dig his way down to it.

In China, where thought finds no support in identity or Being (and thus not in adequation with essence either), it is "constancy" that undergirds the ordered engendering of things and thus regulates the world's process (whence came the very notion of the world as a coherent, undeviating process). And yet here, on the one hand, we find the depiction of characters relegated to another register, where constancy, and thus consistency, is due strictly to an imposed outer form. The resulting uniformity of de-

---

1. In other words, stripping away the learned theological allusions and allegories that for centuries had been fundamental to European art. [Translator's note.]
2. *Zhongguo hualun leibian* (abbr. *Leibian*), ed. Yu Jianhua (Beijing: Zhonghua shuju, 1973), 47.

piction is the same as it would be for simple objects. It leaves no room for painterly initiative, whether of intelligence or of explorative powers. On the other hand, opposite this easily circumscribed composite inventory of standards and norms, among them the human form, we have the inexhaustibility of landscape, of "mountains" and "waters," and their generous distribution of pairings. We have both mountains in their variety of grain and vegetation, with their rocks, bamboos, and trees, and waters in their mutable manifestations, with their waves, vapors, and clouds. For there is continuity all the way down the list, from *rocks* to *clouds*. There is a simple difference of compacity. Have rocks not been called "cloud roots,"[3] puffs of cosmic energy coagulating and densifying in rocks but turning vaporously evasive in clouds?

In the whole-in-correlation that is landscape, mountain(s)-water(s), there can be no resemblance. Resemblance becomes impossible once landscape arises out of the internal "coherence" that sets it in tension—the internal coherence that allows it to soar and keeps it alive. Hence the process that engenders the world will not be reduced to—reified in—any static form. Rocks are no more subject to an imposed form than clouds. A rock (a cloud) can take *any form whatsoever*. What promotes a rock or a cloud to rock or cloud status is that "through which" it attains internal coherence. This is the source of its consistency, and thus of the "constancy" that makes it "viable." And this is what the painter paints. In the words of another great contemporary man of letters, Mi Fu, "in general, for oxen and horses as for characters and objects, copying is enough to capture a resemblance,"[4] whereas for "mountains and waters" a copy falls short. If one "imitates," it "does not come to pass." This is why when it comes to landscape, mountain(s)-water(s), "it is a high place where the workings of the spirit manage to attain themselves."[5]

Even in China's very first pictorial theories (Xie He, in the fifth century), it is repeated ad infinitum that the first principle and chief requirement of painting is that, through painting, we attain *soaring* and *vitality*. Or, to use the associated terminological pair to which the Chinese tradition has ever held fast, it is to attain simultaneously both "breath-energy" and "internal resonance," the polarity known as *qi yun* (气韵): from which proceed "life and movement," *sheng dong* (生动). Thus China presents us with what at first blush seems a paradox: it is not the depiction of a character, not a face (consider, by contrast, what Vasari says about the *Mona Lisa*'s apparent liveliness), that best conveys the *animating tension* from which life springs,

---

3. Tang Dai, *Huishi fawei*, in *Hualun Congkan*, ed. Yu Anlan (Beijing: Zhonghua shuju, 1977), 249.
4. Mi Fu, *Hua shi* (Cf. *Le Houa-che de Mi Fou*, Bibliothéque de l'Institut des Hautes Etudes Chinoises, Paris, 1964, p. 37), §24.
5. Ibid.

or that sustains life. For nothing unitary, nothing isolated, can succeed in this. Such a depiction would reduce to outer traits, and traits, not being *held in tension* by a polarity-forming *other*, ossify at the surface. They are doomed to fixity. To reverse our formulation, it is only by correlation, by the opposition/association of factors, by communication between these factors, and through an exchange between them that we can accede to life. Mountains and waters are no more subject to imposed form than rocks and clouds. But if we trace their twists and turns, follow the sinuous contours in their ceaseless transformation and pairing, as far as the eye can see, the privileged expression—the *site*—of an unquenchable *vitality* will come into view.

2

With the painting of landscape attaining its plenitude in China, the great eleventh-century painter Guo Xi, like the poet Xie Lingyun before him, could think about painting only by deploying the pair "mountains and waters." On the one hand, he says, mountains are "great" or "vast" things; on the other, water is a "living" reality.[6] But why does he call mountains great and vast things? Less because they are sizeable, of course, than because they are stuck with no particular form. They contain the most varied silhouettes and attitudes, never bogging down in any of them. To think of (to paint) a mountain is to think of (to paint) the compossibility of the configurations that keep it aloft in its soaring, by molding and modulating it from its various sides. We are no longer to perceive the mountain as a given, set shape, like a fixed relief, but as invested breath or energy, in ceaseless renewal through crinkles and links of endless variety. Everything proceeds from breath-energy, *qi* (气), which deploys "between Heaven and Earth." The mountain, in its continuous lineaments, is the physical configuration of this. We need only consider that in the Chinese language the lines of force that traverse the relief and hold it in tension go by the same name, *mo* (脉), as the pulse-transmitting arteries of the human body.

But we should read further to learn what the painter expresses as he refrains from seeing in this a simple allegory or personification of the mountain. Indeed, whosoever rightly considers the mountain perceives a conjunction of various thrusts, which in myriad ways hold the mountain in tension. Isn't this what Cézanne knows, or what he does? Indeed, *form* is not the right word here. We would more properly speak of "form-actualization" (*xing*, 形), to borrow the full-on parataxis of the Chinese

---

6. Guo Xi, *Lingquan gaozhi*, in *Hualun Congkan*, 22.

language. Chinese lays out a chain not of (purely visual) aspects but of allures and potentialities. This *actualizing form* of the mountain, it is said, "tends to stand emergent," "tends to impose itself arrogantly," "tends to develop broadly," "tends to squat as it splits," "tends to spread as it spills over," "tends to deploy in consistency," "tends to spring forth dignified," "tends to refine itself in spirit," "tends to assert itself in solemnity," and so on. It would be facile to think that in the foregoing chain the painter is content to humanize (poeticize) the mountain by metaphorically ascribing to it our faculties. He does, however, capture its various modes of intensity, show it to be so many contrasting, interlinked capacities. If we take into account that China was thinking in terms not of "being" but of vested "capacity" (the notion of *de*, 德), we can better understand that the mountain, under its countless pressures and tensions, is the "broadest" and most diverse of physical condensations.

Lacking an imposed form, like rock, the mountain is the dynamic concretion of all possible form-actualizations. Ordinarily the form of a "thing" excludes other forms (it is either round or square), but in the mountain all forms can coexist without conflict. All at once the mountain stands, imposes itself, deploys, squats, spreads, and so forth. Here "broad" means passing up no possibility. Or else, as the painter continues, the mountain "tends to look both right and left," to "extend its greeting one way or the other." It "tends just as much to have cover above it as to have something to climb onto before it"; "to have something before it to prop itself up on and something behind it to lean against"; "to consider from on high as if gazing down"; or "to move about below as if leveling a standard." What I call *compossibility*—the act of entertaining all possibilities equally—is a resource, an unquenchable *fund of forms*, belonging to the mountain. It falls to the painter to exploit this.

3

China, as if wary of subsuming anything under the concept's generality and verticality (what, then, would the "being" of the mountain be?), has had the insight to open this variation up to the realm of the sensible as widely (horizontally) as it can. All of the mountain's *propensities* oppose and respond to one another, and come under tension through contrast. We mustn't bury beneath a typological flourish (the "Chinese-style" encyclopedic inventory that has amused everyone from Borges to Foucault) what is here occasioning the most radical divide and therefore bears serious consideration. China projects no metaphysical "beyond," because it does not split the world (in the Platonic way) such that the intelligible

(Being) in-forms the sensible,[7] and such that the sensible amounts to a mere reflection of the intelligible. It therefore makes sense that China should apprehend the world by laying out the range of possible form-actualizations as finely, and exhaustively, as possible—the range by itself deploying the entirety of the sensible. Thus Chinese formulations—as any given phrase will show—naturally bespeak the world in a *phenomenological* (and not ontological) manner. Hence, too, the Chinese penchant for serial, diversity-exploring inventories. *Con-sistency*, which has no grounding in unitary essence (in what a concept abstractly defines), is thus to be found *within* what it *holds together* through compossibility—what it lists, what it enumerates—of all discerned cases.

The *mountain* is the manifestation, the locus, of this exploration, but the same holds true for its aforementioned counterpart, *water*. Water is said to be a "living" reality because its form-actualization "tends to be deep-calm," "tends to be soft-smooth," "tends to be broad-overflowing," "tends to be whirling-swirling," "tends to be thick-greasy," "tends to be spurting-splashy," "tends to be gushing-shooting," and so on. It "tends to spill over in numerous springs" and "rush forth and pierce the sky" just as it tends to "spray and penetrate the earth." So many possibilities account for the *con-sistency* of water, like a color chart spread to its fullest extent, though the hues correspond less to water's forms of "being" or properties than to its *capacity*. Or else, as our painter goes on to say, water "tends to see to the happiness of fishermen," just as it "tends to see to the festiveness of vegetation," "tends, through fogs and clouds, to draw forth seductive beauty," "tends to draw resplendent clarity from the glen bottoms where it gleams," and so on. Thus in its many different manifestations, binding one thing to another and spreading fertility through and through, water is indeed the "vehicle of vitality."

I linger over this concept of *consistency* in order to elucidate in "what holds together" (what is "con"-"sistent")—in what will not be corralled into the unitary, reduced to *essence* or idea—a mode of comprehension of things that *stands apart from ontology* and can itself be understood only by correlation. What I am calling *con-sistency* refuses to be ranged under "Being" or, to put it differently, refuses to lay spurious claim to metaphysical support. It stems instead from the *co-he-rence* thanks to which the one depends on the other and will not be isolated. What we call landscape draws its consistency from the correlation of mountains and waters. The mountain, it is said, deploys the course of the water, and the water *animates* the mass of the mountain. Chinese thought never tires of varying the pair through a crossing of registers. The mountain, continues Guo Xi,

---

7. Etymologically, to inform is to give shape to (in-form). Jullien uses the word in the special sense of "give meaning to." [Translator's note.]

has water in the way a body has "arteries for the circulation of blood," and water has the mountain for a "visage" or "face." Moreover, it owes to the mountain "its charm and seductive power."

In its rocky mass the mountain is also, says Guo Xi, "the skeleton of Heaven and Earth." This skeleton "has the virtue of being solidly and deeply anchored" and "not to appear on the surface." The water, meanwhile, is the "irrigation of Heaven and Earth." This irrigation "has the virtue of flowing from all sides," "and the course never condenses or clogs." It is from the coupling of the two—from the *stable* rooting of the one and the *fluid* flow of the other—that the world deploys. In this respect landscape, mountain(s)-water(s), could very well be painting's vocation and even that through which we can attain reality in its *entirety*. But "reality" is a clumsy word for this, hobbled as it is by our substantialist bias, the bias of *res* and "thing-ness" and the very bias that Chinese painting-thought, in exploring the correlation between mountains and waters, is forever undoing.

4

Should we suddenly feel lost amid these many correlations, should we tire of this play of "mountains" and "waters," should we wish to take back the reins and steer our way back to reason, or should we wish to find some fulcrum that would best condense the jointly vested choices—or let us say, rather, the biases—in both the landscape painting and the landscape-thought of Europe, I think it natural for us to appeal to *perspective*. A theoretical (heroic) invention, perspective is the peg on which Europe long ago set its truth to depend. At the very least it distills, both conceptually and technically, all the particulars known to us of European thought's encounter with landscape. In perspective the primacy accorded to visual perception is imperiously asserted. It takes the solution of the "open window" to its definitive extension: the entire frame of the painting ("an open window through which I see what I want to paint," as Alberti put it[8]). By retaining only the observer's point of view, at the visual pyramid's summit, perspective instantly posits landscape as "ob-ject," requiring the "objectivity" of its representation. Before such a representation the Subject comparatively—supremely—measures and determines its "truth." Moreover, perspective strips space of encumbering significations and then proportionally divides the homogeneous expanse, "tiling" it, to construct its *composition* geometrically within it.

---

8. From John R. Spencer's translation of Alberti's *On Painting*. [Translator's note.]

From the Renaissance onward this sort of perspective went hand in hand with landscape's emergence in European painting. As we look within European pictorial art itself, however, we can *already* attest, by the same token, that landscape asserted its autonomy at last and achieved full expression in European painting-thought (from the Impressionists to Cézanne) by gradually loosening perspective's grip throughout the nineteenth century and then bursting suddenly free by that century's end. Thus in our approach to landscape we arrive at the following question: was the perspectival construction helpful—was it a good entry point—for landscape's accession and deployment? Or was the invention that brought landscape to light in Europe an obstacle to landscape's apprehension? What alternative might we have to the optical device that perspective established as a necessary mediator (Alberti's gridded "veil" or "intersection"[9] between eye and object) but whose fallacious truth—that is, lazy convenience—we have spent more than a century denouncing? What could we do besides substitute its mere opposite, or abandon it, or displace it? As we all know, revolution, even pictorial revolution, remains forever in debt to the very system it so noisily overturns.

Given the foregoing, we might consider, on the other side of the divide, how Chinese painting-thought promoted remove in painting. For the painter we have begun to read, Guo Xi, there is not one, exclusive perspective—exclusive as singular truth contrasts with numberless error—but *three* collaborating modes of "remove" (*san yuan*, 三远).[10] By correlation, once again, these modes deploy the landscape in conjoint dimensions and confer on it their *con-sistency*. Through them we are *immersed* in the landscape. *Deploy* is, in fact, the apt term, for "without a deep remove it is superficial," says Guo Xi in a new series. "Without flat remove it is near"; "without high remove it is low."

To state things positively, "raising your head from the foot of the mountain to the mountain's summit is what we call high remove"; "standing in front of the mountain and looking through it to what lies behind is what we call deep remove"; "contemplating distant mountains from nearby mountains is what we call flat remove." Suddenly all notion of an eye fixed before the landscape as before a window is gone. We needn't transpose a unit of measurement (Alberti's arm length) to produce a distance proportionally, or situate a single point on which to pivot our central radius. Nor, consequently, need we draw transverse lines from this point to determine the spacing of our figures and, finally, lay down our *compositio*. To the complementarity of viewpoints there correspond instead three manners of looking: "raising the head" (*yang*, 仰), "penetrating with the

---

9. Ibid. [Translator's note.]
10. Guo Xi, *Lingquan gaozhi*, 23.

eye" (*kui*, 窺), and "contemplating from afar" (*wang*, 望). Looking is not neutral, or unitarily abstract. Rather, it modulates and distributes itself as we move between our various positions. "Volume" is no longer conveyed all at once, through the optical contrivance of diagonal lines converging on a vanishing point and bringing about constructed "truth" as if through an instantaneous face-to-face. Instead, volume is conveyed as the eye, ranging *processually* about, discovers the landscape from various angles: from below, from in front, and from nearby.

The landscape's "atmosphere," meanwhile, varies simultaneously. The atmospheric perspective of the Italian painters only abets mathematical perspective, for it nonetheless divides distance into clear-cut grounds (green close in, brown further off, and blue at the horizon). For Chinese painters, by contrast, atmosphere is born of our three dimensions, none taking precedence over the others. "The tonality of high remove," in Guo Xi's parallel, "is limpid and clear"; "that of deep remove is heavy-dark"; and "that of flat remove alternates between light and dark." Also, "high remove's lines of force are bold and resolute"; "the feeling of deep remove is expressed through layering"; and "the feeling of flat remove is expressed by nebulous vapors dissipating to infinity." The depiction of figures varies in consequence: "in deep remove it is delicately fragmented"; "in flat remove it is a pale blur." These coordinates suffice to integrate figures into a landscape; figures do not provide the "measure" or standard (man as the "measure of all things," the great Greek theme if ever there was one) for the rest of the landscape. "Standing out clearly, [the depiction of figures] is not [too] high; in a pale blur, it is not [too] big."[11] Far from bowing to a single demand, aptness of depiction remains relative to each of the "removes" by making them cohabitate.

5

The Chinese painter says nothing further about this, and perhaps nothing further will ever be said in China. In the Chinese view this is but a painter's proposition, meant neither to stand as a principle nor to serve as a demonstration. Truth is not at stake here as it is for Alberti, who is advocating the right method and refuting other methods. The Chinese way thus gives us no sense of having at long last glimpsed the reason of things. We have not now achieved mastery over "things" by transporting them safely from one order to the other, in keeping with the laws of optics. A "painted thing" can seem equal to a "true thing," as Alberti says, only "at a specific distance." This is to say in consequence that neither will

---

11. Author's brackets throughout the quotation. [Translator's note.]

we feel the emotion or satisfaction of having made a discovery; we will not feel the Albertian (European) sense of wonder at having penetrated a secret or having produced a "miracle of painting," *miracula picturae*. The Chinese painter-thinker, for his part, lays no claim even to originality. He is, we repeat, content to put correlations into play, with delicacy and precision, so that, as one thing pairs with another, everything responds to and intensifies everything else, and no possibility goes to waste.

Indeed, the reason that the Chinese conception of landscape does not start with an individual-subject facing the landscape as an observer is that the center and axis of said landscape is the mountain itself, in its variety and "breadth." It is the mountain that "has three removes": from its base, from in front, and from the nearest to the most distant mountains. Rather than have the mountain passively submit to the eye by spreading evenly before it, the Chinese manner has "perspectives" emerge as a function of the mountain and of its *compossibility*. It is not that the three ways of deploying remove are incompatible; instead, it is that none takes primacy over the others. Rather than compete, they concur. Their conjunction plunges us into "three dimensions." What we have stumbled upon is, at any rate, a hitherto-unnoticed approach to "3-D" that dates back a thousand years.

That there is correlation rather than exclusion here we can more easily appreciate in the return to polarity. Landscape, in Guo Xi's summation, both "comes" and "goes" (*lai qu*, 来去). It spreads and folds back on itself, condenses and unfolds. We minutely scrutinize and vaguely contemplate it. It presents itself "head-on" and askance:

> Head-on, torrents and mountains, woods and forests curve and tangle: thus disposed the landscape comes; we do not tire of its detail, and the eye delights in its proximate quest.
> Askance, in a flat remove, peaks and summits multiply and cluster: thus interlinked [the landscape][12] goes, dissipating; we do not tire of the remoteness, and the eye opens to the far bounds of the vastness.

Between the poles of near and far landscape is simultaneously appearing and disappearing, bringing and taking away, and imposing itself and escaping us. No "presence" is left to coalesce, no "essence" (*ousia*) left to stand apart. There is no assignation to confer immobility—and thus no possible ontology. It is like a wave that spreads and dissipates, enveloping the eye, every eye, in its telluric ebb and flow. In this back-and-forth the landscape mobilizes. In this coming-and-going, this influx-reflux, landscape gives rise to *respiration*. To cite a phrase of recent currency in

---

12. Author's brackets. [Translator's note.]

our part of the world (we must determine what ambient displacement it is symptomatic of), it is a *paysage* "à vivre," a landscape to be experienced, or lived.

6

On this very note Guo Xi begins his *Treatise on Landscape*.[13] He gets right down to business, opening with the fundamental question (indeed, the only question that matters): "Where resides the good man's love for mountains and waters?" Once more the parallel formulations of the reply weave a web of affinities in which we are instantly immersed. There is landscape through the redeployment of poles and the tensions that arise between them. A landscape, I repeat, advenes through what it *mobilizes*:

> Hills and crops: to feed his landed nature
> — here he seeks always to dwell;
> wellsprings and rocks: to whistle carefree
> — in this he always delights;
> fishermen and woodcutters; to withdraw in solitude
> — to this he always tends;
> monkeys and wild geese: to fly-cry
> — this is the company he seeks always to keep.

From the start landscape deploys in what we will call—in as yet too rigid (too tabular) a fashion—a "living environment." Rather than a perceived landscape, it is a milieu and a "set of surroundings." It is a place where we sojourn, we stroll, and we neighbor. There we are in our *element*. What thus gives rise to landscape overall, to use the charged Chinese verb—the verb that spans the gap from physiology to ethics—is that we "nourish" our life on it (养生). What *finds nourishment* in landscape, in other words, is not only—not restrictively (physically)—the body. Nor is it the "soul" (in the figurative, metaphysical sense: "nourish" the soul with "truth," says Plato). It is, rather, "breath-energy" (*qi*, 气), the very thing that circulates "between Heaven and Earth," the mountains and the waters. Or inversely (here Guo Xi draws from old Taoist formulations), in landscape we free ourselves of "disgust" (of "lassitude") for the world's "dust" and "din," for its vitality-squelching "chains" and "fetters." As we nowadays like to put it, landscape is a place where we can "revitalize" ourselves.[14]

---

13. The work is commonly known as *Treatise on Mountains and Waters*. With this translation of the title Jullien is doubtless pointing out, once again, that the correct if nonliteral rendering in European language of the Chinese term *mountains and waters* is in fact *landscape*. [Translator's note.]

14. The French language—the original reads "*on s'y 'ressource'*"—allows Jullien to hark back to one of his key terms: *resource*. [Translator's note.]

"Revitalization" is a term very much of our time and has yet to make it into the dictionary,[15] though our misgivings might stem from its use in advertising slogans. I myself distrust its use by the purveyors of personal development, who peddle a mythical brand of health: the myth, that is, of a natural state purged of all artificiality. What I dislike, to give it a simple name, is the false naïveté of this. And yet in landscape "revitalization" suddenly finds—discovers—a proper use. For the purposes of our Chinese thinker the word is justified and suitable. As Guo Xi himself hints, through a veil of learned allusions that soften the acerbity of his thought, he puts his faith in neither of the following two possibilities. On the one hand, these immortal sages "ringed with nimbuses and clouds" are indeed the object of our "aspiration," although we "do not manage to see them." On the other, we have political life; if times of good public order, under the authority of a "Prince" or "Father," ought to quell our temptation to withdraw from the world, what are we to do at present aside from sacrifice ourselves heroically, like the greats who have come before us?

In this ideological reckoning of his condition (if I may risk expressing it in terms proper to our own times) our Chinese scholar finds no solid ground on either side. He has neither constructed a "faith" in transcendence, structuring the "Invisible" (trusting to the salvation of some God), nor erected a form of citizenship, a *civitas*, for his political—historical—exercise. He neither "believes" nor partakes in the promotion of any sort of "Progress." The only "capital" (already in Xi Kang we find the Chinese term 资 being used in this sense) to exploit therein lies in his "vitality," the only hope in his longevity: "long life" (*chang sheng*, 长生), not eternity (which takes Being and identity for granted). Nor does he separate the ideal from the vital, and landscape ends up being the very locus of this *nonseparation*.

Guo Xi connects with these polarities, deployed on the very surface of the mountains and the waters. Escaping the fetters of the social, he allows the mountains and the waters to activate and mobilize him, and thereby raise him to full "capacity." (To convey the same idea today we speak of being in "great shape," a familiar phrase that, in passing, nullifies the opposition between "soul" and "body.") In so doing Guo Xi makes landscape not into a decor, not into something pleasantly bucolic, but into the very thing from which his sole possible bounty—his life—can, through renewal, well up. Thus "revitalizing" himself, he can once again soar. He can draw breath and energy. As landscape shows, the world, down to its very physicality, is made only of "breath" and "energy" (*qi*, 气), which flow or coagulate. Guo Xi's "quest," in other words, is for neither Truth

---

15. The French term used here, *ressourcement*, is indeed generally defined in the etymological sense of a "return to the source or origin" rather than as the sort of replenishment one might seek on holiday. [Translator's note.]

nor Liberty, the two great absolutes that Europe has zealously held up for so long. It is for "mountains and waters." This is also perhaps why Europeans, returning from the great investments of yesteryear, have taken such an interest in landscape.

7

But what are we to do, Guo Xi now asks, when we are physically deprived of "that aspiration to the woods and the springs," when we have left behind "the fellowship of murk and fogs"? We can return to these things "at night in our dreams," but "our senses are cut off from them." This is when the *resource* of painting makes its appearance. "We need only find a marvelously deft hand" and "it will bring this forth in profusion." "Without leaving our mat or stepping down from the room," "keeping our seat," we will be able to "go explore the springs and ravines." "Monkey cries and bird calls will continue to fall silently upon the ear." "The gleam of the mountains and color of the waters will captivate our eye with their surge of light." Our painter-thinker concludes with an encapsulation: "How can this fail to satisfy our inner verve, fail to ravish our mind?"

If we consider that, in the established lexicons, *represent* (*représenter*) is the French term most commonly associated with *landscape*, ahead even of *see* (*voir*) and *paint* (*peindre*), we might more easily understand, by contrast, what a landscape "to be lived" means, barring the way as it does to the aforementioned imitative path. This is not a matter of representing "a" landscape by reproducing the *aspectual* through *mimesis*, the Greek choice that has attained classical status in Europe. Instead, it is a matter of using the vim of the brush to bring out the *vitality*, the play of affinities and correlations, of *all* landscape—of landscape as mobilizing environment—in terms of both what falls on the ear and what ravishes the eye. Instead of "looking at" a painting (as "spectators"), we undergo the experience of immersing ourselves, and even of losing ourselves (*qiong*, 穷), in the tensions between mountains and waters, "springs and ravines." Is this an "aesthetic" pleasure, as the West has categorized it? No. It is, rather, a gratification of *living*, through the activation it provokes. At the beginning of his *Critique* Immanuel Kant calls it *Lebensgefühl*—though he subsequently allows it to get lost under the aegis of the "beautiful," under the apparatus of the "object" and its "representation."

Note, however, that beauty is never at issue with Guo Xi. In his pages the term *beautiful* (*schön*) is never applied to landscape, for it would remain on the surface. And where does the value of a landscape lie? Guo Xi goes on to tell us, resorting to a standard classification: when it comes to landscapes, "mountain(s)-water(s)," there are those that one "traverses";

those that one "contemplates from afar"; those [in][16] which one "strolls"; and those in which one "dwells." But the landscapes that one traverses or contemplates from afar "are not worth" the ones in which one wanders at leisure (*you*, 游) or in which one enjoys a sojourn. There is as much difference between "traversing" and "strolling through" as between "looking at from afar" and "dwelling in." The difference, of course, is that the former remain external, whereas the landscapes in which one likes to stroll or dwell become *milieus*. They are ambient; they are *imbued*. There one is in one's *element*. And so we now take the further step of acknowledging that what gives rise to landscape is irreducible to the perceptual. Rather, it promotes itself into a locus of *exchange* and makes the landscape *intensive*.

---

16. Author's brackets. [Translator's note.]

IV

When the Perceptual Turns Out to Be Affectual

1

Landscape will not be reduced to the perceptual. Rather, it establishes itself as a locus for exchange. This is evident within landscape itself, where the correlation of mountains and waters becomes the chief polarity, but we can see it also in the correlation of the "self" and the "world," of "physicality" and "interiority" (let us begin with this least psychological of terms). The boundary lifts between the inside and the outside, both of which enter into polarity and become permeable to each other, and the result is a new "interspace" [*un nouvel « entre »*].[1] The exterior that lies before my eyes emerges from its indifference and neutrality. "Landscape" arises from such coupling. There is landscape when I *feel* at the same time as I *perceive*. Or let us say, rather, that I thenceforth perceive inside myself as well as outside myself. The hermetic seal that sustains me as an independent subject blurs. To state this new definition of landscape more categorically, there is landscape when the *perceptual* turns out to be *affectual* at the same time.

This has gone oddly unacknowledged in Europe's landscape-thought. Or if we have known it, if we have *lived* it, have we thought it? That the perceptual should, by landscape's effect, split in two or be endowed with affectivity has utterly escaped our concept of landscape, utterly slipped through its cognitive net. We have known it "intimately," in our innermost selves, in some recess of our being, if we have "known" it at all.

---

1. In Jullien's philosophy the interspace (*l'entre*)—literally, the between—is the space opened up by the exploratory divide (*écart*) between cultures. [Translator's note.]

Recall that landscape is defined only as "a part of the land that nature presents to an observer." Such an arrangement permits no "interspace" to lead from one to the other. The two terms are kept aloof from each other. At best, mention has been made (rarely) of (bucolic) "charms"—the "countryside"—"offered up to the eye." But does this refer only to charms (ornaments)—that is, only to a surplus: the famous and shopworn "bigger soul"[2]—added to the uniform realm of the perceived and the heard? In Europe landscape is understood at best only within the category of the pleasurable or agreeable. To delve into the origins of this deafness we will have to trace European thought backward. We must undertake to de-psychologize it, and de-subjectivize it as well.

We must also specify how and under what conditions the perceptual and the affectual come to be knit together in the *interspace* of landscape. What offers itself up to perception must, first of all, belong chiefly to the physical, at the level of the inorganic. We approach such "physicality" (I borrow this term—the most general term—from anthropology) in its breadth and its separateness, without the privilege of a human tie or singular link with a "self." We have traditionally, and most generally, called such physicality "nature." As we see in painting, we might encounter human beings or other creatures, but they are secondary. In like manner God "adorned" the world of his Creation, *opus ornatus*. The quickening effect of this is all the greater because we are dealing with another kingdom, indeed with the "other" par excellence. We are dealing with the *nonhuman* taken as a whole. Paradoxically, then, what stirs our sensibility is itself the height of insensibility. We cannot on principle permit ourselves the slightest acquaintance with it or even hope to bring the perceptual near, for there must be some remove; there must be some distance between us and it. For there to be landscape something inaccessible, a beyond, must subsist.

The thing that touches me in what gives rise to landscape is not what is not human. Nor, to state it negatively, is it the inhuman. It is the *nonhuman* par excellence. The nonhuman is independent-indifferent and can therefore in no way be resorbed; it cannot be the object of desire and cannot be consumed. We have refused the fruits of the orchard. And thus "beautiful," because gratuitous, because it disconnects pleasure from interest, can recover a measure of aptness. In other words, landscape arises when this *exteriority*, which remains most irreparably marked (this is why, as Romanticism posited, there must be wilds in landscape), lends

---

2. Literally, a "supplement of soul [*supplément d'âme*]." The notion comes from Henri Bergson's *Two Sources of Morality and Religion*, whose standard translation (by R. Ashley Audra and Cloudesley Brereton) reads, "We must add that the body, now larger, calls for a bigger soul, and that mechanism should mean mysticism" (310). Ashley Audra and Cloudesley Brereton (Macmillan and Co., London, 1935, 268). [Translator's note.]

itself to internal perception while also prompting us to discover within this "interior," in the depths of a "self," an interiority that we have never suspected—an interiority that has lain dormant (buried) and unstirring. Landscape prompts an otherwise mute core to resound. (Stendhal: a landscape is like bow [drawn across the strings of his soul].[3]) A landscape "touches" us not accidentally or anecdotally but essentially, because in its pure exteriority it causes us to feel an inner kernel of self (more inner than "self"). It reveals *the intimate* within me.

Here, moreover, the perceptual, because it grafts itself onto landscape's physicality, is *durative*. Landscape does not move, does not "flinch." It is in the instant "always there." It therefore connects us with another temporality, shifts us into the lastingness that resides within it. Should we come upon a landscape all of a sudden, in an instant, the time that follows does not count. We might go so far as to say that said time is abolished. The "at the same time" of perception and affection is an unending development. Our simultaneous sinking into the world's physicality and into our self's intimacy cannot be hurried. Nor can it be exhausted. Though we cut loose from landscape (turn away our eye)—indeed, we are bound to do so at some point—landscape's *resource* remains inexhaustible. We will tire of a place, of a "view," perhaps, or of a "spectacle," but never of a landscape.

A further consequence: because we are dealing with physicality and not with the human, because physicality is what enters into the partnership, the *induction* from one to the other (here too let us state things phenomenally, not psychologically) is completely modified. The *perceptual-affectual* here is not a matter of passion and pathos. It is rather their exact opposite. Would it pertain even to the emotions? Do we in fact understand how to conceive the opposite of *pathos* in terms other than those of impassivity? Can we give it a name? Is it even amenable to specification? This is why I have spoken of the "affectual" and not of affect—of a *pure* capacity to let oneself be affected and not of affects, which always entail the plurality of the diverse. Diversity's range of options, by inviting us to make a choice (joy/hardship, etc.), would mask not so much the ambiguity as the mute and diffuse tone of the affectual. The relation we establish with landscape is not limited to some pleasure or typical satisfaction. (Does "pleasure" even enter into the picture? Here, once again, we ought to distinguish landscape from the "beautiful.") The relation sounds a fundamental, preliminary harmony. It does not produce a distinct sound so much as put us in tune with a coevality (the self—the world) that is just starting to reemerge.

---

3. "*Les paysages étaient comme un archet qui jouait sur mon âme.*" From Stendhal's *Life of Henri Brulard*. [Translator's note.]

2

If I must specify the coupled items that are engaged by landscape, or that *between* them prompt landscape within me, then I will start by distinguishing the perceptual from the *perceived*. The latter is too limited and determined (this or that thing coming into view at such and such time). It is too factual, too anecdotally given, and thus too accidental. As long as the *perceived* is in play we have a place, a view, or a spectacle, but not landscape. But the perceived is also not the *perceptible*, which meets the perceived at its limit, considers perception only at its edge, where already it stands under threat from its opposite and at the limit of its possibility. We must understand the *perceptual* from a categorical point of view. It should evoke all that is amenable to perception, and we should therefore not need to actualize perception completely or to perceive everything individually. It is not by hearing/seeing in detail that I enter into landscape. The perceptual has to do with perception globally mobilized as a fund or *resource*.

The affectual, meanwhile, should also be understood in a global, categorical way. The perceived elicits only "an" emotion. With landscape, however, induced emotion defies complete individuation. It retains a measure of vagueness and indeterminacy. It is a state of sensibility (of vibration, in more elementary terms) that is awakened without our being able to pinpoint a cause, without our specifying it or giving it a proper assignation. It deals less with a particular sentiment, like the sounding of one pitch instead of another, than with an *emotionality*, or tonality, that responds, that spreads, *below all emotion*. (This is more easily expressed by the English word *mood* or the German word *Gemüt*.) There is landscape when an inner receptiveness is so thoroughly roused that it is disencumbered of all singular objects or thoughts. For this reason it is a matter not of an "affect" but of the *affectual* as a capacity—a more primordial capacity—to be affected.

However, as we can see at least in its definition of landscape, European thought, as if crippled, has struggled to consider the *perceptual* and the *affectual* conjointly, as a natural pair, in the way landscape demands. On the one hand, thanks to the primacy of vision, the perceptual has from the start found itself turned toward abstraction and following the path to knowledge. From the perspective of classical philosophy my senses interest me only insofar as they inform me of the world, collecting rhapsodic knowledge that my mind can then "order" and "synthesize" (Kantian understanding). On the other, the affectual has been considered only with respect to behavior and morality. The question now becomes how I can manage (dominate) my affects, for subjective affectivity is apt to disturb one's normative reason and cause it to veer off (a line of thought that reaches its apogee in Spinoza). Moreover, the perceptual and the affectual have been kept apart by the split that has occurred in European philosophy, one to either side of the fracture. (European philosophy considers knowledge *or* action, Truth or the Good—"What can I know?" or "What ought I do?"—as two separate planes fated to join together.) Landscape-thought found itself stuck and as it were flattened in the powerful jaws of this theoretical vise. Only the passive "observer," for the purposes of knowledge, was retained.

When at last another field opened up, the field of aesthetics (Kant strikes again, forging ahead brilliantly with his third *Critique*), the debate (the "beautiful" versus the "sublime") continued to address landscape from the sole angle of the "faculties." Here the understanding, reason, and imagination serve as the vertices for a triangle of possibilities. The connections between them can vary, or else enter into "free play," but we never shift away from the Subject's perspective and initiative. We have still not left behind the separation of the self and the world, the notion of a world *facing a subject*. The question of landscape is now ranged under the (strictly subjective) question of "taste" and "judgment," the master categories. We still cannot tackle the question of landscape on its own merits, respecting its proper vocation and using the proper tools. To embrace that possibility we must not keep redoubling our efforts (make ever finer distinctions). We must not keep constructing and "going beyond" (the *forging ahead* that keeps European philosophy ever vigorous). Instead, we must proceed to *undo*. We must "deconstruct" yet more of our reason and regress from it. We must delve *further beneath* the conditions of possibility and into the folds of our thought, so as to unfold it—and thereby open it up to landscape.

In saying that landscape advenes when the perceptual reveals itself to be affectual as well I automatically set aside the sovereign function of a Self-subject. It occurs *between* "self" and "world," and I am not the author. In fact, I am neither passive nor active, and neither more than the other. These categories (the categories of European grammar) fall apart on their own. To describe this, then, we must forsake the province of the self's autonomy and enter that of "influence," as one might speak of magnetism (however contrary being "under the influence of" might be to the prerogative of individual-subjects who pride themselves on their "liberty"). Or else we must enter the province of "induction," as we have recently begun to do, and as one might speak of it in, say, physics. In other words, we must enter the province of flow and imbuing, of propagation and attraction, and of waves and intensity. We leave behind the categories of psychology, based as they are on a subject's faculties and initiative, and consider what "happens" as stemming from pure *phenomenality*. We do this not because we seek to steer the process back to more "objective" knowledge but because—if we hope not to break the continuity from the perceptual to the affectual, and if we hope not to interrupt the exchange between "world" and "self"—we can grasp the reactiveness within me only as something that itself belongs to the world. For that is what a "landscape" is. Landscape is what tears down the boundary within which the Self autarkically (psychologically) withdraws and renders that Self to the world in the moment.

3

Landscape offers itself up—or, rather, forms—in the moment. It is for the most part influence and propagation, ambiance and diffusion. And it is such already at a physical level: trees with waving branches, light that suddenly breaks through the clouds. All of this is evident in another pair that gradually emerged within the Chinese language, established itself in parallel with "mountains" and "waters," and became the other approach to landscape. It too conjoins two factors or two dimensions, brings into play the complementarity of opposites, and brings a correlation to bear. The Chinese language gives us "wind-light" (*feng jing*, 风景) or, in its four-term expansion, "light (calm) wind—lovely (pleasant) light" (*feng he ri li*, 风和日丽). Whereas "mountain(s)-water(s)" speaks to the correlation of High and Low, of the stable and the shifting, of what imposes a solid form and what is formless, or of what is seen and what is heard, this other pair—which slowly advanced, no doubt in search of greater coenesthesia and momentaneousness, until it settled into "landscape"—speaks to the association between, on the one hand, the invisibility of passage and penetration (*wind*) and, on the other, the diffusion of visibility (the *light* of the sun). Whereas mountains and waters establish landscape in its *consistency*—in both its physical "breadth" (the "mountain") and its "vitality" (the "water")—the correlation of wind and light, once semantically sealed, carries its quest for landscape to the very surface of landscape's sensible manifestation. *Wind-light* seeks out landscape in relation to passing time, imbuing itself with landscape's mutability and luminosity.

Suppose that instead of "landscape" we said "wind-light." "Wind": the wind is such that we feel its breath but cannot see it. It conveys indefinitely in its course, but we observe only its effects. "The wind passes, and the grass bends,"[4] says Confucius's good man. The people feel the influence emanating from the Wise Man's character, but they feel it unawares, through discreet imbuing. For the wind is what filters in through

---

4. In Arthur Waley's translation: "When a wind passes over the grass, it cannot choose but bend." [Translator's note.]

the smallest opening, snakes through the slightest crack, and pervades all things equally (cf. the trigram *xun* in the *I-Ching*). Wind designates the impulsive dimension that traverses the *structural*—what is firm, solid, and constitutes the frame of things—and keeps the structural *soaring*. This is so as soon as we make use of language (and in Chinese reflections on literature[5]). With respect to a text's "skeleton," which is essentially semantic and rigorous in its determinations (*gu*, 骨), the "wind" dimension is what makes a text "vibrate," what renders it shifting and communicative, by deploying its "import." It thereby develops meaning and conveys the author's "incitement" to the reader (his receptor), who finds himself penetrated and carried away.

Let us consider *wind* not only as a strictly atmospheric (meteorological) element but also as the *propagating* modality par excellence: the modality that, in traversing, gives rise to the *interspace*. "Wind" is the course or continual current that links and spreads. If we consider that "wind" is, in fact, China's oldest poetic rubric (and the title of the first section of China's first anthology of poetry, *Guo Feng*, 国风, which dates back more than three thousand years), we instantly see how early China quickened to something that in the West drew scant attention: the transmission of an influence all the more effective (imbuing and pervasive) for being impossible to grasp or apprehend. In and of itself such a concept of "wind" *undoes* (dissolves) all thought (ontology) of autoconsistency or own-ness, of the isolated or hermetically sealed, of essence and the assignable.

Viewed as "wind," landscape comes to be thought of as *diffusion* and not merely as density: as a discreet, not altogether appreciable *influx* and not merely as patent and tangible. In China wind prompts us to think of landscape in terms of its variation as well. Since earliest antiquity the Chinese have distinguished "eight winds" (*ba feng*, 八风), by provenance and direction. The "wind" known as "luminous" (*feng jing*, 风景) is warm and mild. It is this wind, through its semantics, that favors (fecundates) the advent of landscape. The Chinese—for lack of categories founded on essences or properties (in the ontological manner)—have characterized each of the four seasons by its predominant wind. In like manner, "wind" is here the ordering but dynamic principle, classifying without substantializing. It both orients and differentiates. China has thought in terms of rubrics and registers, but not of Being and identity.

Within landscape the diffusing, penetrating, invisible "wind" finds a counterpart in the spreading, inundating "light" of day, which renders visibility. But light of this sort also allows for an alternation of brightness and shadow. It does not spread obstinately or parch. (In the golden

---

5. Liu Xie, "Feng gu," in *Wenxin diaolong*.

age the same term meant shadow as well, until shadow was graphically distinguished.) The pairing developed such that wind was declared to be "mild" ("gentle") and light declared to be "lovely" ("pleasant"). Accordingly, there was landscape when their correlation prevailed without violence, when its effect was to bathe in fluidity and luminosity, to *imbue* and *clarify* at the same time. That it was not coercive made it all the more effective, and thus wholesome for the lives of beings. Landscape bespeaks "wind-light" in its ambient tonality, in its delicate touch, which affects all manifestations of existence indifferently and lifts them to an outpouring. It thus promotes itself to the status of scene and singular moment (promotes itself, as English aptly puts it, into *scenery*).

We can corroborate this in the moving passage to follow, without a doubt one of the first (and rare) instances in Chinese literature where "wind-light," that other name for landscape, stands in vis-à-vis with "mountain(s)-water(s)" in order to mark a separation from it. The "scene" dates from the early fourth century, when the Chinese court, harried by invaders from the north, was compelled to flee and seek refuge south of the Great River, in a landscape of hills and lakes where at that very time landscape poetry and painting were flourishing. "Every lovely day" gentlemen gather in the countryside, stretch out on the grass, and feast. One of them suddenly sighs: "The wind-light is no different [from when we were up north],[6] but if we raise our eyes, the mountains and the waters are other." "And all looked at one another and let their tears flow."[7] Landscape as imbuing influence, as ambient sweetness, had the same intensity, but its physical and even political consistency had shifted.

We might have expected the change to occur in the momentary influence, but it turns out that transitory (ephemeral) imbuing too is characteristic of landscape. We find it in era after era. This semantic pair that develops in the Chinese language highlights the manifold connections of something for which we in Europe have but a single word. The scene—in its tonality "of wind and of light," in its unanimous vibrancy, in its mildness and harmony, and in all the ways we allow its gentle penetration—has indeed retained its previous tenor. It is as it was before we were compelled to flee our country, before the hardships began. We are just as keen to go out and break our fast outdoors, "on the grass," in our preferred company, and sensible to the charms of what now so intimately gives rise to landscape. What has changed is the frame. The "mountains" are no longer the same. Nor even is the "river," or indeed the historical conditions. The moment's landscape quality is the same, but the times that give the world its *consistency* have changed.

---

6. Author's brackets. [Translator's note.]
7. *Shishuo Xinyu*, chap. 2, "Yan yu," §31.

4

One of the resources of Chinese language-thought is an ability to recompose pairs and form new correlations at leisure. "Light" (*jing*, 景) can synthetically retain the meaning of "wind-light" (*feng jing*, 风景), denoting landscape's tonality, and then itself pair off with a new (and assonant) counterpart: our "nature" or "emotional" capacity (*qing*, 情, itself drawn from the pair *xing qing*, 性情). Here "(wind)-light" denotes an overall "sensitive exteriority" to which "(nature)-emotion" denotes a "reactive interiority" as its correlate. To use our previous terms, "(wind)-light" bespeaks the *perceptual*; "(nature)-emotion," the *affectual*.

Bringing this new pair into play—especially with the great seventeenth-century thinker Wang Fuzhi—Chinese thought on the phenomenon of poetry now trained all efforts on demonstrating that fertility lay only in the cooperation of its two terms, and that the two were inseparable. For "landscape" forms not only in the world, outside, among things over there, at the focus of their forces and forms, in their consistency as "mountains" and "waters," and in their play of "wind" and "light." It advenes *between* those poles, the poles of the "self" and the "world," of interiority and exteriority, and in the reciprocity that develops between the one and the other. Thus the perceptual reveals itself to be affectual *at the same time*. In more unitary terms, landscape is *perceptual-affectual*. To say it in reverse, if perceptual and affectual do not connect or correlate, (a) "landscape" does not advene.

We can now better appreciate the usefulness of the Chinese theoretical apparatus. By looking at *everything* in terms of correlation it breaches the walls behind which Europe's psychological (insular) notion of the self-subject lies entrenched. It thereby also closes the rift between what "we should call [the] soul or something else," as Plato said, and the world's physicality, a dissociation that renders indecipherable the compenetration from which landscape arises, or at least renders it paradoxical ("Inanimate objects, have you, then, a soul?"[8]). But how are we to grasp a *nondissociation* if in fact grasping entails isolating? How, in other words, are we to *conceive* of something not by separating it, as we are taught, but by doing the opposite: by undoing the very possibility of separation?

The advantage of Chinese analysis—or of what exists in its place, which is not "analysis" (by "decomposition") but continual *pairing*—is that it invites us to consider in terms of pure phenomenality "what happens" ("where it happens") when landscape takes shape, when the soul casts no shadow and the subject's position has no bearing. It invites us to consider

---

8. From the last line of "*Milly ou la terre natale*," a poem by Alphonse de Lamartine: "*Objets inanimés, avez-vous donc une âme / Qui s'attache à notre âme et la force d'aimer?*" [Translator's note.]

landscape as a *process*, a process of exchange and interaction, between poles that suddenly enter *into phase*, between instances (interiority and exteriority) that come into accord and induce each other. Consequently, Chinese analysis has the far-from-trivial merit of delivering us from bad lyricism, from the attempt to compensate for the schism between the poles—a schism due to the objectivation of physical knowledge (the knowledge of the "observer") by a pathetic and "romantic" subjectivist surplus. For all its bloat, the surplus cannot patch over the schism. Rather than enlighten, it bogs us down. It clings to our language and gums up our pens as soon as we in Europe mention landscape.

The Chinese thinker, meanwhile, holds strictly to the play of correlations and the phenomenon of *induction* thereby established: "Landscape is to emotion [or the perceptual is to the affectual, 关情者景][9] as amber to straw"[10]—a Chinese way to speak of magnetic phenomena. In other words, a *field of attraction* opens such that neither remains isolated from the other and the separation is erased. "Although emotion and landscape are distinct insofar as they deal with interiority or the materiality of the world," he continues, "it is nevertheless the case that landscape engenders emotion and emotion engenders landscape." Result: "incitement to sadness or joy" and "the extended welcome of blooming buds and stars turning out" "come to rest [store themselves] within each other and trade their dwellings" (互藏其宅). The process initiated between these poles—between sentiment naturally aroused and the world's physicality—is thenceforth inexhaustible. To imagine their "exhaustion" when it "[goes] in the direction of joy or sadness," when "an interaction is produced that never ends," and when there is "a current that goes unobstructed" is to "understand nothing."

The Chinese thinker has no need for a "soul," does not posit a self-subject. (Indeed, is there even a "Poet" here?) In truth, there is no subject to these correlations other than the perceptual and the affectual. Although the relationship is conceived as a process between sensible interiority and the world's physicality, nothing leads us to suppose that the accord between them is unequivocal. In such a poem two verses evoking the landscape's grandeur and magnificence might be answered by two verses evoking a personal sense of aging and abandonment.[11] The correlation between landscape and emotion remains open, able to shift from one meaning to another, "joy" or "sadness," "with nothing suitable or unsuitable." There is nothing rigid, predetermined, or codified about it. The correlation is constantly establishing itself and available to all inflections.

---

9. Author's brackets. [Translator's note.]
10. Wang Fuzhi, *Jiangzhai shihua*, ed. Dai Hongsen (Beijing: Renmin wenxue chubanshe, 1981), 33.
11. Ibid., 34.

This has nothing to do with "the lid and bottom of a chest," says Wang Fuzhi (who claimed that, through overuse, this particular correlation had in recent Chinese poetry become mechanical and stereotyped). For this reason the matter at hand, to speak in my own terms, pertains not to "affect" (this one or that one, each excluding the other) but to an *affective fund* [*fonds affectif*].

5

How can we speak of the compenetration of landscape and emotion, of the perceptual and the affectual, if indeed we cannot distinguish the one from the other, if each thereby loses its identity? Our Chinese thinker has a pet phrase for describing how far the demarcation's undoing extends. There is, he says, "fusion-imbuing," or "liquefaction-imbibing" (*xiang wei rong jia*, 相为融浃), such that he can vigorously declare, "Emotion and landscape are two, as terms, but are in fact indissociable."[12] When there is "landscape," in other words, the distinction between perceptual and affectual becomes purely nominal, ceases to be in any way effective. Indeed, this is how we gauge the presence of "landscape."

We find evidence for this in landscape poetry (although it is admittedly true that all classical poetry in China tends toward "landscape poetry"). In the highest poetry the accord is so "naturally/marvelously obtained" (妙) that the frontier between the two vanishes. In poetry that is merely well crafted there is "landscape in the emotion" or "emotion in the landscape."[13] At any rate, the mark of a good poem is that in this accord between emotion and landscape, with the poetry proceeding simultaneously from the one and the other, landscape is attained in the moment; it is grasped suddenly and spontaneously in equal measure. Indeed, we need no longer hesitate between this and that word (*xian liang*, 现量; in Buddhist terms, *chan*: the "such as it is" of an emerging "present").[14] What gives rise to landscape is our having forsaken all supposed mediation, whether of reason or of projected sentiment, because mediation obstructs the encounter. We forsake even all consciousness or property of a "self." We accede at last to the *immediate*, and thus need no longer wonder whether it corresponds to the "self" or to the "world."

That the rift between the "self" and the world should suddenly vanish or collapse to allow landscape to advene; that a connection should be established or a tension set up, through the "self," between interiority and exteriority, such that they become partners; that I should thus perceive

---

12. Ibid., 72.
13. Ibid., 72.
14. Ibid., 52.

myself phenomenally, not as a psychological agent but as a factor, as the intimate counterpart of an environment that allows itself to be taken in indefinitely; and that we should therefore no longer need to bother connecting the psychic to the physical—none of this, despite any fears we might have had, turns out to be due to any "materialist" reduction. What justifies and explains the encounter within landscape is not that the "self" yields its "spirit" quality (or, inversely, that the world is "spiritualized," for neither ought we to personify nature). It is, rather, that the "self" and the "world"—the individual and subjective, on the one hand, and "mountains" and "waters," as well as "wind" and "light," on the other—can enter into correlation, because in the Chinese view they stem from the same "reality." As I have said, however, this reality is not that of *res* or substance. We would have to say "what" it is without resorting to "Being." This reality is such that it can in fact permit a transition from the physical to the spiritual. As a result, it is such that we can speak plainly, without metaphors or doublings, and without any overreach, of a landscape's "spirit."

V

✝

When "Spirit" Emanates from the Physical

1

How do we advance through this obvious minefield? I am not certain there exists at present a more unwieldy, more suspect term than *spiritual*. There is no denying that I am venturing into risky territory. There is, in truth, no term more compromised. And yet could we do without it? Let us not shy away from this brutal but salutary question. After all the Hosannas of moral injunction (the famous "spiritual values" of the past), we cannot help but cast a skeptical eye on so much consensus and piety. Indeed, we might yet fear falling into the resilient ideology, succumbing to "spiritualism" (good old "asceticism"). How, moreover, are we to speak of a "landscape's spirit" without resorting to the expedience of cleaving the world in two and opting for the "physical" or the "metaphysical," two realms kept apart, with one at best serving as the other's "salvation"? In other words, must we speak of a "landscape's spirit" in the same sense as we say that a hill is "inspired," that is, in the sense that the Spirit comes from elsewhere—from a Beyond hidden from view—and descends on the mountains and the waters like the dove in a church painting?

Or else are we positing a metamorphosis, engaging in facile personification, when we speak of a "landscape's spirit"? Are we indulging ourselves, admitting a twinge of emotion, a little daydream, or a tweeze of vibrato? Are we, that is, smoothing our rough oppositions out a bit, after the fact, by veiling them in poetic rags? I have already denounced the *subjectivist surplus*, that affectual escape valve for the great objectivation of the world undertaken by physics. What we have, then, is essentially a decorative phrase, a gentle malapropism that offers a halo to compensate for the hairs we have split (the traditional call for "literature" to paper over what science has laid too bare). Needless to say, we will not be taking the expression seriously. We will not be reading it literally or ascribing to it some possible truth. We expect no "revelation" to come forth. Truth be told, we fail to see in it even a reasonable object of thought.

Yet as we lay out and catalog the various meanings of *spirit* in our languages, as we plumb the word's resource, we suddenly make out a sort of dissonance, perhaps even the remnants of possible dissent, or at any rate something like an asperity. There is indeed no harm in agreeing on the word's theological (Hebraic) sense, in which the "breath" or spirit of God (*ruah*) "moved upon the face of the waters," and on its philosophical and originally Hellenic sense, in which the spirit (*noûs*, νοῦς), as immaterial being, stands in detachment from the body and hence designates the activity of thinking. But what are we to do with the third sense, now all but extinct, because buried by the two others: the nearly silent, extinguished, obsolete sense of "emanation of bodies" ("subtilization" of things)? It barely survives now in certain local usages, like "spirit of wine," "spirit of salt," or "spirit of perfume." Here the word refers to the product of a decantation, to what is *exhaled from the physical* in its indefinite deployment and to what turns vaporous, like a subtle emanation, but *does not separate from the physical*. The phenomenon of the *aura* is not brought to bear or added on (fake); it is one with the thing.

2

This almost forgotten meaning is perhaps a thread we can follow on our way into landscape. This sense that we observe on the eve of its plowing under, this relic of an abolished rational system prior to the great rise of science, is no vector or engine of dualism. Rather, it alone labors, discreetly, for dualism's undoing. It is stubborn and resilient, drawn straight from experience that we cannot deny and can repeat as we like. However tenuous, it momentarily reseals the great cleaving of the world. It surreptitiously reestablishes a connection between tangible physicality and what lies beyond. Whether we speak of wine, salt, perfume, or, now, landscape, "spirit" emerges as an extension of physicality, not as a break from it. It proceeds not from detachment or miracle but in a processual manner. In this *aura* the sensible slips past its limit but is never forsaken. Though we call it obscure, archaic, or the stuff of an intolerable alchemy, this "subtlety" or "quintessence" spans the gap between the opacity of things, substances, and bodies and the field of expansion (of activation) that emanates from it.

This cast-aside meaning of *spirit*, which now crops up only sporadically, like the vestige of some former way of life that modern science has relegated to the unthinkable, and which I am so gauche as to adopt for my language, is something we will have to recover, whatever the cost. It has put us onto the scent of some forsaken thing, but what? It was actually *necessary* (equal parts legitimate and heroic) for modern science to bury this meaning, so as to legitimize its own conquering rationality in the struggle against "obscurantism." And today, now that science's foundational dualism has exerted its great clarifying effect, we must rediscover the *possibility* beneath the term's peremptory disjunctions, so that further on we can exploit its *resource*, and thereby "recover" a capacity that modern science has induced us to cast aside: the capacity to dwell in the world and live in—or, rather, "off"—a landscape.

This, at any rate, is where a rigorous rethinking of "landscape" leads us, even if we must reconsider our past exclusions, unfold and recast our language, and conduct a series of de-categorizations. For we cannot see, or cannot *experience*, how landscape is no longer a strict matter of "land" unless it is specifically the place where the world's physicality manages to extract itself and deploy. Landscape is where land breaks with the limits of the sensible, flares out, and "emanates" as an *aura* beyond its tangible form—although without abandoning its texture, its singular anatomy of "mountains" and "waters." It is from their active correlation, as from the play of "wind" and "light," that the "spirit" thus emanates. It does so, then, without setting itself up as a Beyond that lies removed from the sensible and more conveniently—"rationally" (in a way that lends itself to model-making)—becomes operative.

"Landscape," taking a detour around our experience, has now unexpectedly reestablished a connection between things we believed we had definitively separated as isolatable entities, namely, the "physical" and "spirit." Transcendence deploys effectively within—or, rather, through—this connection, but in an eminently sensible way, without divorcing itself from the physical, and thus without demanding some *other plane*, whether theoretical or theological. The "physical" and "spirit" come into accord. I would even ask, in return, whether in this regard landscape did not play a compensatory role in our modernity. If we so cling to landscape these days, is it not because, falling short perhaps in our self-analysis, we resort to landscape (find succor in it) to express, under the guise of "literature," our suppression of the grand dualism on which Western science has thrived?

Let us not be afraid, at least not at first, to *unfold* what we have hitherto considered forever *folded*. Let us not be afraid to drag some old terms out of the shadows. There issues from the sensible an "exhalation," a "decantation," and a "quintessence." As it intensifies it loses opacity. It flares out or becomes *evasive*. Such is the *aura*. I will have to cleanse the term "evasive" of its negative connotation, of its dubious, uncertain sense. In thus reapplying the word to things, in rehabilitating our language, returning it to former customs, I can use it to convey the phase at which the sensible pours forth, breaking free of its constraints and limits. In spilling over, the sensible can go beyond itself, can become "emanating," and can emit "spirit"—be it flavor of wine, scent of flowers, or landscape. A landscape's "spirit" dimension, then, stems from *emanating* and *evasiveness*, two concepts that we must substantiate as we go along. If we do otherwise, if we confine "spirit" to its intellectualist sense, we will likely fail to understand what gives rise to landscape. We will stroll blindly past its *resource*.

3

My new definition of landscape, in parallel and in response to the previous one, will in fact be the following: there is landscape not only when the boundary between the perceptual and the affectual is erased, or when the perceptual is revealed to be, at the same time, indissociably affectual, but also when the breach is sealed between the tangible (the physical) and the spiritual, and when spirit *issues from the physical*. In other words, landscape's peculiarity, what promotes it from land to landscape, what causes "landscape" to arise, is that it hoists us—lifts us—to that transition and makes the transition apparent. Landscape elevates us into the spiritual but does so *within nature*, within the world and our perception of it: that is, within the world of mountains and waters where I dwell and stroll, through its alternation of the solid and the fluid, the visible and the audible, and the opaque and the transparent. There is landscape when the world, through the activity of its correlations, clears out and opens op [*ouvre du dégagement*][1] within itself and compels us to experience it. *Clearing out and opening up* is the key term. For nowadays (here is our new philosophical task) we must not so much renounce transcendence (all thought that sinks into its negation dies) as stop thinking of transcendence as flight (into some other world). We must think of the "spiritual" no longer as "Being" (in opposition to the flow of becoming) but as something processual. In this sense landscape is *revelation*.

Thus we can better understand why China was the first civilization to think of and give a name to "landscape," and why in the eyes of Chinese thinkers landscape became nothing less than the place where the "revela-

---

1. This special term means to clear out obstructions (conduct a sort of housecleaning to get rid of clutter and all things unnecessary) and thereby open up the possibilities (unfold the folds, to use another of Jullien's images). [Translator's note.]

tion" occurred, its very locus. China never carried the distinction between the sensible and its beyond into a metaphysical split, and was therefore at leisure to conceive of the spiritual's deployment as a phenomenon, as occurring *within the physical*. Landscape is the locus of a flaring out and a going beyond that remains within the world. It is an opening unto the infinite within the finite (*of* the finite). Remember, the most basic term with which Chinese thought approaches what we call the "real" designates both that from which beings and things proceed materially and the flow that goes through them and keeps them aloft in their soaring (*qi*, 氣). Landscape, then, is where the opposition breaks down between "matter" and "spirit." The term's primitive glyph evokes the shape of a cloud and is later thought of (written) as the vapor of boiling rice. Such a term was apt to keep us in the transition from the perceptible to the imperceptible, at the stage of evasive soaring and its emanation.

This is a commonplace in China, because it is among the most elementary notions. It inspired not the slightest doubt at least until the encounter with the West and Western science. Did China even perceive a bias in it? The following passage, among many others, reiterates the foregoing. It starts with the original Great Void and ends with the formation of landscape, the correlation of mountains and waters:[2]

> Breath-energy [氣] deploying as the original Great Void rises and falls, and constantly shifts:
> such is the nature of the empty and the full, movement and repose, the start of yin and yang, of the hard and the malleable.
> Floating and rising: such is the limpidity of yang; sinking and descending: such is the confusion of yin.
> Through incitement and communication, gathering and dispersal, form the wind and the rain, the frost and the snow, the continual flow of existences without number, the fusion-concentration of mountains and waters.

Although this is the most general of texts—a sketch in broad strokes of the origin and process of beings and things rather than a meditation on landscape—landscape is where the text logically arrives. It arrives at the major correlation: between "mountains" and "waters." In their physical advent, proceeding from that incessant play of interactions, "mountains and waters" are the global and legitimate manifestation of the broad soaring from which the world springs. More exactly, yin and yang are the two opposing and complementary modalities—the poles—of matter-energy (*qi*, 氣). Yang, the propensity to rise and decant, brings matter-energy to "limpidity" (清), and thus to "spiritual" elevation, whereas yin, the propensity to descend and coagulate, leads to sedimentation, making

---

2. Zhang Zai, in *Jinsilu*, compiled by Zhu Xi, chap. 1.

matter-energy heavy and "murky" (浊), and thus gives rise to the opacity of things. Moreover, it falls to landscape, as it sets the world forth in the breadth of its correlations, to bring to light this process-by-immanence, even though, as we read further on, there is nothing, not even "lees of wine or ash from the hearth," "that does not teach" of it. The play of these tensions, activated in landscape, is *naturally* "refined" into "spirit" (精神). And this "spirit of landscape," just as it proceeds from no Beyond but instead emanates through its tangible forms, does not harken to another world through its *aura*.

4

The "biography" on him in the *Standard Histories* reports mainly that our scholar loved hills and rivers and so enjoyed long walks that he would "forget to come back." With his wife, who shared his "love for landscapes," he scaled Mounts Jing and Wei, to the west, and Mount Heng, to the south. On Mount Heng he decided to build a house. In the hard times that followed, with his family too impoverished to help, he began farming the land to subsist. He was offered, we are told, the post of director of registers and turned it down in terms deemed sufficient: "For more than thirty years I have haunted the mountains and drunk from the rivers of the valleys." The emperor himself approved of this reply. Later, still refusing this or that official post, he returned to Jiangling and said, "Old age and illness are upon me, and I fear I will never again see the famous mountains. I can do nothing but seek to purify my inmost self and contemplate the Tao as I lie in bed and walk about within." He also "painted at home all the places he had hiked." These were utterly new paintings in his time. During the day, reclining with a lute, he would always face those landscapes.[3]

What can we make of these gleanings of his life (of which we can hardly learn anything further)? What should these few words conjure in our minds except that his life was lived entirely in landscape, that it was a life condensed in and absorbed by landscape? Here, I think, the aforementioned "off" is no longer so far fetched. We may trot it out and say that our scholar "lived off landscape." His "thirst" for the beyond and the infinite, if we remain on the level of the vital (we are indeed dealing with *vitality* here), finds fulfillment in landscape; he thus never tires of his life, for once within landscape one lacks for nothing. Having sworn off once and for all the earthbound ambitions of politics, he finds in "mountains and waters" a *clearing-out and opening-up [dégagement]* outside worldly strictures,

---

3. According to the biography in the *Songshu*, chap. 93.

a way to get beyond all exiguity. In and through landscape he aspires to emancipation from the world, but this emancipation, though achieved through tension with the "beyond," does not steer him toward another world. The flaring-out of the landscape is enough. It allows him to evade the world's closures and confines, and thus its ability to thwart, squelch, or frighten. Yet we are told that after the death of his wife, whom he was known to hold dear, he turned to Buddhism, then making its way into China. But he never did as Petrarch did. He never, as it were, grabbed his copy of Augustine's *Confessions* and scaled Mount Ventoux (Europe's first ascent to be recorded as such) to deplore from its summit, in the name solely of conversion to God, the vain "spectacle" before him. The Chinese scholar's experience was the reverse: it is in and through landscape that he accedes to transcendence.

More than a scholar, the man in question, Zong Bing, was one of China's first painters, living in the fourth and fifth centuries (375–443), and wrote the first treatise on landscape painting, which is but one page long. (The work attributed to Gu Kaizhi is more the description of a painting than a treatise.) This was certainly the world's first text to blaze a trail toward landscape-thought. At the very least it appeared more than a thousand years before Europe formed the notion of landscape.[4] Right away, the first sentence is decisive: "With regard to landscape," "mountain(s)-water(s)," "there is materiality but / such that it tends toward the spiritual" (质有而趣灵, in which the median term, 而, is an "empty word" that signifies both concession and consequence). Landscape is indeed made of "physicality" but in such a way that it is aspirated into a spiritual dimension. This is why landscape is essentially a form of soaring, an impulse, and a going-forth; this is why it is alert rather than inert. The physical and the spiritual are distinct, but we are always going from one to the other, and doing so *via* the landscape. With respect to the materiality of things (质) the other term, *ling* (灵), denotes the undying, tension-keeping aspiration. This is why our experience of landscape is the great initiator, why the transcendence operative within landscape is *instantly* revelatory.

In truth, though, how can landscape in and of itself be the setting for an instance of "transcendence"? (Are we not perhaps resorting to a linguistic convenience—of the sort so often abused in the past?) How can landscape not just point at transcendence with a sign but actually take us into transcendence? Zong Bing replies by probing what tensorially (inexhaustibly) gives rise to landscape. He evokes "Mounts Song and Hua." There transcendence is indeed captured. It is constantly at work and available to our perception, but it is irreducible to a "spectacle." On the one hand, the

---

4. *Hua shan shui xu*, in *Zhongguo hualun leibian* (abbr. *Leibian*), ed. Yu Jianhua (Beijing: Zhonggua shuju, 1973), 583.

mountains are distinct, eminent, and resplendent, carving their haughty shapes (秀) out of the light. On the other, they also contain in their dark slopes the vacuity of the primordial, gloomy like the womb's recess. They contain the "spiritual animation" of generative power (玄牝之灵), as Laozi calls it (§4). Landscape, with its peaks and valleys, with its gleaming summits and shadowy vales (*yang* and *yin* originally referred to the adret and ubac of a mountain), is the apparition of the world-tension that *opens the way* to our passage beyond the world. Ridges emerge and jag, dazzling in the light and taking individuation to its zenith. Meanwhile forms in the shadowy valleys have yet to achieve separation and bathe in their inherent confusion. Within landscape itself we have fathomless background, the font of flows both matrical and material, and the source of the world in its continual transformation. Thus landscape plunges us physically—or, better yet, phenomenally—"between Heaven and Earth" (天地之间); it plunges us raw into the fundamental interaction that endlessly promotes existence and conveys us to a *clearing-out and opening-up*.

5

And so we get closer, *through landscape*, to what the "spirit" is all about— or, better yet, to what is "going on" with the "spirit," with the soaring and infinitude that landscape carries within, in its very physicality. For one thing, "spirit" is, in man above all, what "finds itself moved" and is promoted at every encounter with the countless incitements that weave together in landscape. "Spirit" at that point "transcends" (神超), Zong Bing continues, and the "principle inherent to things is attained" (理得). But is spirit confined to the qualitative rarefaction-heightening of *breath-energy*? No doubt because already under the sway of Buddhism, Zong Bing takes this line of thought—potently conductive and generative as it comes to us from Laozi in particular—and opens it to the immateriality of spirit (thereby bringing us closer to *spirit* in the European religious sense). Here once again his words are delicate. I will try to render them without resorting too much to our expected terms: "Spirit is fundamentally without bounds [that would make it appear] [神本亡端]: it takes shelter in sensible actualizations [栖形], giving rise to correspondences [感类], [such that] the principle of things penetrates shadows and traces [理入影迹]."

Here, *in landscape*, we find ourselves, I believe, on the brink of metaphysics. We are as close as can be to the separation between two orders of reality but without crossing the line of demarcation. We are thus not proceeding to the *break* that gave birth to metaphysics. The distinction does not lead to a cleaving of the world, and we can therefore simultaneously consider both sides: both the transcendence of the Spirit and landscape as the sufficient manifestation—here and now, in the moment and with no hint of a void—of that transcendence. We might try to meet this double exigency by remedying the lack of technicity in the use of ideas—Chinese thought does not bother with this (and therefore sees no problem in it)—but two things happen with the spirit if we take the trouble. First, the spirit, becoming absolute, withdraws from the phenomenal and "takes root" in a deeper level of sensible actualization. Second, in its continual soaring, the spirit "takes shelter," "takes up lodgings," in the sensible; this gives rise to correspondences in the sensible, which in turn prompt communication through the sensible, with every singular individuation bearing the "trace." Thus landscape—because it is always opening correlated factors onto each other, because it actuates polarities—is what *naturally* manifests this "transcendence" of the spirit, maximizing its scale and intensity.

In the immanence from which it proceeds, landscape carries the *transcendence* of Spirit. In other words, the vocation of the landscape-thought that emerges in China at the dawn of the fifth century is to penetrate the absolute but without breaking with the world's immediacy. Such, indeed, is landscape's "import." Landscape amounts to religion, so to speak. It wades into religious waters, but it also substitutes for religion, by delivering us from dogma and from belief in an Elsewhere. Landscape is from here but shot through with the beyond. Chinese landscape-thought is crucial, then, because landscape is what opens physicality and deploys it—*flares* it out—all the way to the Invisible. Better still, let us trade our overly substantive (ontological) "is what" for the ever-so-common Chinese motif of the "way," or the Tao. Landscape is that *through which* the bottomless depths of the Invisible, in its soaring, becomes eminently amenable to the senses.

Moreover, we can think of landscape if it serves as our link between two terms: *the physical* and *spirit*. And we should doubtless choose to be mindful of this link as we read the following gem of a phrase, from Wang Wei (415–443), landscape's second great thinker: "What takes root in physical actualization melts spiritual-ness [within itself]" (本乎形者融灵).[5] All by itself the term *melt* (with its triple meaning of liquefy, blend with, and amalgamate) bespeaks the mutual penetration that yields indivisibility even as the solid fluidifies. It is the term par excellence that does not separate and that bars the way to dualism (the opposite of Plato's famous "cut," *temnein*, τέμνειν). It is also the term that, in its substantive (descriptive) form, denotes the warm vapors that in Chinese landscapes rise from valley floors, making contours nebulous and dissipating into *aura*.

---

5. Wang Wei, *Xu hua*, in *Leibian*, 585.

Enter poetry, notably the poems of someone we have already met, to say the same. A contemporary of our aforementioned painters, Xie Lingyun (385–433) was China's first great landscape poet. In the play of his correlations between mountains and waters we note his attention to the "spiritual animation" (the same term as before: *ling,* 灵) "manifesting itself" in landscape. This time the mountain evoked is not streaming with water in its "arteries" but looms amid the waters of the Great River and is lapped by the current ("Scale the solitary Peak in the middle of the river"[6]):

Cloud	sun	between	shine upon	reflect
Air	water	together	purify themselves	refresh
Manifesting animation	spiritual beings	[among the]	no one	to appreciate [it]

"Between," "together" (at the center of the two verses): elements in an accord that prompts their communication and exchange, that frees each from its thing-ness (from its *slack*, nonsoaring character). What henceforth gives rise to landscape is the fact that physicality is no longer mired in itself, in its opacity. Now it radiates and allows itself to be traversed (the sun—the clouds); it decants and turns limpid (air and water). Transcendence—discreet but always at work (discreet because always at work)—lies in the promotion that opens unto the other and carries us beyond what in itself becomes sterile (reifies), in its property. Landscape "manifests" ("exteriorizes," 表) it, says the poet. Is there, in fact, a transcendence other than the one that continually deploys itself by immanence within the sensible and promotes the sensible? For proof, concludes the poet, observe that all the "wise men" (the glyph here, 仙, stands for man and mountain) vanish into the distant mountains, breaking free of the causal chain that binds existences; there they manage to "nourish the life" within them to its terminus and become almost "immortal." But there will be no dream of "eternity" for them, as we have dreamed in the West, because in China there is no support to be had from Being and identity.

6

Examining the notion of the *aura* remains troublesome, even after Walter Benjamin. When it purports to designate a body's emanation—what subtly escapes from a substance (the "subtlety" of the alchemists) and renders it diffuse—the "aura" involves more than just some old, obsolete,

---

6. "Deng jiang zhong gu yu."

readily dismissed physiology of "fluids" or "breath." And when it claps a halo onto certain bodies, a halo visible only to believers, the aura verges dangerously on the occult. It is a vague expression of the very thing for which the thought of distinctions—the kind of thinking that the West has overwhelmingly come to embrace—reserves its keenest disdain, not to mention disgust: to wit, *vagueness* itself, evasiveness, and nebulosity, which can be neither isolated nor verified. In other words, it defies classification on either side, with the visible or the Invisible, and instead dilutes the boundary between them. It is what thereafter belongs to neither order, to neither the physical nor the spiritual, and does not separate the two. We speak of ambiance, influence, or atmosphere—of all that diffuses and sets no bound. In like manner the *aura* refers back to what Being-thought most loathes—to what escapes the grasp of determination, and thus also of essence and assignation. It refers back, consequently, to what Being-thought hopes not to trouble with.

But the image of vapors rising from the vales, blurring and melting away the relief and its forms, gradually dissipating into the sky—a vision common to the entire Far East—requires the notion of the *aura*, precisely because the aura undoes circumscription and definition, and undoes markedness and ontology. It speaks to the way in which landscape opens onto a beyond of the tangible, dissipating its dead weight. This "beyond," however, is no "elsewhere." Thus we never in fact depart from the tangible. There exists a "flavor beyond flavor" (味外味; Sikong Tu, ninth century) to which the term *blandness*, by registering minimally in the sensible, best lends itself. This flavor-beyond-flavor develops indefinitely by breaking free of raw sensation, which is marked and therefore limited. In like fashion there is, as they say in Chinese poetry, a "landscape beyond landscape" (景外景). "Blue fields [under] a warm sun: from the lovely [buried] jade a mist rises. One can contemplate it [from afar] but not put it exactly before one's eyes."[7] In literal Chinese, landscape *exhales* (exalts in) its physicality, because, by becoming less dense (less massive and less compact), it *intensifies*. And by intensifying it promotes itself into landscape. It is not abstracted from the concrete (does not rebuild itself on the plane of intelligibility, as in the work of our Cubist or so-called abstract painters). Instead, it is extracted from its concretion, like perfume from flowers. It is "subtilized" and "imbues." It *decants*, that is, by refusing to be confined to any materiality whatsoever.

A certain Chinese phrase, which has since entered the lexicon of landscape painting, can help us think through the notion of the *aura* more carefully. There is landscape, runs the phrase, when the landscape's

---

7. Sikong Tu, "Yu Ji Pu shu," in *Zhongguo lidai wenlunxuan*, by Guo Shaoyu (Beijing: Zhonggua shuju shuju, 1979), 1:500.

physicality ceases to serve as a barrier, when its opacity dissolves, when it allows itself to be traversed by a tension that goes beyond it, and when the resulting sensible animation spreads in every direction. The terms, translated one by one, go as follows: "actualized form" (形), "animating tension" (势), "influctual (or energetic) dimension" (气), and "phenomenal manifestation" (象). Let us for once not hesitate to disturb a neat table and break it down analytically (make conceptual use of it). An "actualized form" is what is individuated in a physical configuration. "Animating tension" comprises the lines of force running between a landscape's actualized forms and deploying them. The infused "breath-energy" spreads throughout and keeps them aloft in their soaring. "Phenomenal manifestation," finally, bathes the entirety of the landscape, expressing it physiognomically and conferring the thing we struggle so hard to speak of (and to grasp): the "air" (ambiance and atmosphere)—the atmosphere of a landscape, as we might speak of the "air" of a face.

These terms sometimes occur in pairs: "form-tension" on the one hand, "atmosphere" and "tonality" on the other. This is something along the lines of a relief's movement, and something of the moment, dependent on the weather. "Landscape is the form-tension of Heaven and Earth [形势]; and [the play] of wind and rain, of darkness and light, is landscape's atmosphere [气象]" (Shitao, eighteenth century). More commonly, however, the four terms are used as extensions of one another, as parts of a single, continual process. They thereby constitute landscape in its dimension as "aura." To undo our metaphysics, it is explained—though not without twisting the phrase—that through landscape's physicality (形) there emanate lines of force (势) as vectors (factors) of energy-respiration (气) that deploy indefinitely as a sensible manifestation (象). However, as the painting treatises specify (Guo Xi),[8] this can be understood only at a distance, through disengagement. In like manner, one can apprehend landscape's aura, proceeding as it does from decantation, only at the cost of "purifying" one's inner self. If you approach it in a "spirit of woods and springs," says Guo Xi, then landscape's "value is high." But if you approach it with "eyes of disdain," it will be worthless.

A landscape's "value" stems less from its defined, marked, set traits than from what traverses it, what emanates from it as an effect, what diffuses from it, and what does not restrict itself to it. Or, rather, we must once again renounce the substantiating locution "what is" and amend our language. If we wish to think landscape through, then we must undo the vocabulary (or, better yet, the grammar) of both identification and attribution. We must straddle the distinction between what "is" and what

---

8. Guo Xi, *Lingquan gaozhi*, in *Hualun Congkan*, ed. Yu Anlan (Beijing: Zhonggua shuju, 1977), 17.

"is not," as well as the distinction between the active and the passive. We must do this to pass into (clear a way toward) the undeveloped or suspect register of our languages—the quickly untenable register—of [what] does not "belong," that is, what is not properly "pertinent": the register of what no longer has essence but is nonetheless not the opposite of essence in Greek, the "everything flows" of mobilism; and the register that deals not with "being" but with the *interspace*, with traversing and imbuing, exhaling-infiltrating, or the evanescent-invasive.

7

The decantation-purification that deploys landscape as aura already expresses what is, in the Chinese view, painting's primary trait, the very foundation of its legitimacy. For Zong Bing, the first landscape thinker, it is this trait that justifies the whole enterprise. The Kunlun Mountains are immense, and the pupil is tiny. Bring the eye right up against the mountains, and all sense of their form vanishes. Yet step back, and even so vast a landscape fits within that pupil. The same goes for the vastest mountains set within the tiny compass of a painting. Because a landscape is apprehensible only at a distance, and distance amounts to *a clearing-out and opening-up* [*dégagement*], the landscape itself is "instruction," and more effective than any moralizing. One attains wisdom more surely, says Zong Bing, by painting "cloud-covered mountains" than by "working one's way back" to the remotest classical principles, or "wading" into the infinitely fine subtleties derived from their formulations. If painting, then, is the reliable mediation through which we accede to landscape, landscape is the *reliable mediation* through which we accede to wisdom.

We must hear at last what China tells us about landscape and understand just how radical the message is. We must hear without suspecting the slightest hint of "literary" effect—without pretense or exaggeration. Zong Bing proclaims it from the start (though we can read it only *in fine*): landscape sets us on the road to the absolute, leads to Revelation. In his eyes there is a blatant parallel between the one and the other, the Wise Man and Landscape: between the way of wisdom (as taught by the Buddha) and landscape's vocation (as expressed in painting). The two are set forth in a vis-à-vis:

| The Wise Man | through his spirit | shapes the Way, Tao |
| Mountains and waters | through their actualized form | make the Way attractive |

Landscape does not transpose (because it has no dualism) but relays the Wise Man's teaching and makes it seductive, "attractive" (媚), by expressing it within the sensible. As the preamble already states, whereas the Wise Man, carrying the Way within him, enlightens all beings with his light, the man who purifies his inner self can "savor" the world's phenomenality (味象). Or, as the end of this great page reads, while the Wise Man's teaching gleams over all generations, the ten thousand traits of landscape (万趣) "melt" (within themselves) the thought they inspire. Once again we encounter *melt* (融), the verb that earlier was barring the way to dualism. Landscape, in its continual shifting and in its infinite diversity, "melts" the absolute into the sensible (although by using these terms I have, of course, begun to set things in stone). Landscape incorporates the absolute, blends it, and fuses it.

After all, what is the definitive gist of the Wise Man's (the Buddha's) teaching, once we strip away the ritual muddles and dogmas, as our Chinese scholar proceeded early to do? As stated in the conclusion, it is that everyone can accede within him- or herself to the "nature of the Buddha," and that there is no "Reality" (or Truth or Ideal or Absolute or whatever else one might call it) outside what one "realizes" by "deploying the spirit, and that is all" (畅神而已); one realizes this by breaking free of all ties and adherence, even to one's mind. And what, meanwhile, does landscape make us feel (experience) once we know how to accede to it through a *clearing-out and opening-up* [*dégagement*]? That all that is realized through the correlation of mountains and waters, down to the shape of stone, the rustle of water, and the slightest vibration of "wind" and "light," makes us right away, in the moment, "realize" reality in all its plenitude. Or, rather, makes us realize "realizing"; lets us allow the gerund to speak of the same process of advent, irrespective of the subjective/objective. Landscape occasions the physical emergence of this *realizing*, which is henceforth in no way deficient, because from this point on nothing will ever boast greater existence. Nothing will have greater existence than the "shape of a cloud" (the primitive glyph 气, meaning cosmic energy), at least if one has emitted one's spirit as the landscape decants by exhaling (exalting) itself as aura, set in *tension* and no longer inert.

VI

Tension-Setting

1

Truth be told, *paysage* (landscape) is a dulcet term in French—more so, perhaps, than its counterparts of similar composition in other European languages, where a ruder phonetic transition causes one to trip rather than flow from one syllable to the next. *Paysage* glides right out of *pays* (land), emerging like the chrysalis from its shapeless larval body. "*Pays*"—"*paysage*": "land"—"landscape." I began by criticizing the term's definition in Europe (expanse cut out by an observer's eye) but not its derivation. The semantics have a richness of their own. *Landscape* detaches—clears out and opens up—from *land*'s somber expanse and promotes itself on that basis. The gain in the passage from "land" to "landscape" is not a onetime thing; it is not a gain merely of aspect. There is, rather, a qualification of the whole. We suddenly discover a resource. More than a mere matter of visual pleasure, it is something to exploit as a fund (*fons*: "source"), and I believe it touches on *living*.

This advance was brought about notably by Rousseau, in his great letter on landscape where the lover speaks to the beloved (it is through the landscape as well that he speaks to her in *Julie, or the New Heloise*, I, 23). Rousseau cuts to the quick, beginning with the classic theme of "land," spatial extent, and the observer: "It has taken a scant eight days to cover a land that ought to take years of observation." He completes these few pages evocative of the Haut-Valais by extracting *landscape* from *land*, the latter giving birth to the former: "I will have spent the entirety of my trip solely under the landscape's spell." Even as *paysage* (landscape) starts to rhyme with *voyage* (journey; Stendhal, tightening the adequation, will later say that it was "strictly" for the "beautiful landscapes that I made the trip"), "spell" speaks to the extreme intensity of an expansive satisfaction not to be gotten from a moment's view or a "spectacle." Sensation lifts us to a different, infinitely superior plane, where we no longer hold the initiative. It transports us into a world that we have never expected and have never even imagined. Whereas in China "mountains and waters" (or "wind-light") bespeaks landscape in its *correlation*, in Europe "landscape" bespeaks landscape in its *promotion*.

"Land"—"landscape." Sinologist Paul Demiéville conveyed the transition felicitously when, in his sorrow over the debacle of June 1940, he pondered a famous verse by eighth-century Chinese poet Du Fu (*Guo po shan he zai*) and produced the following translation:

Le pays est brisé, reste le paysage.
[The land is ruined; landscape remains.]

But what does the suffix add in the passage from *pays* (land) to *paysage* (landscape)? The *-age* (-scape) through which landscape deploys denotes three values in French: collectiveness, action, and result of action. Should we not follow common practice and retain only the first? By definition, landscape is an "overall apprehension of the land" (from the dominant vantage point of an observer). In a word, landscape is "assemblage." (Baudelaire: "If this assemblage of trees, mountains, waters, and houses that we call landscape."[1]) In contemporary aesthetics, now under the authority of the sciences of language, this has led logically to landscape's definition as "an assemblage of disjunct and amorphous elements" that "the eye—that is, the mind—gathers into a signifying whole." This can be done, Françoise Chenet-Faugeras concludes, only "on the basis of a subject's cultural and linguistic presuppositions."[2]

Here once again, though, I wonder whether a definition founded, it would seem, on such broad consensus appears obvious only because we have buried and forgotten the biases that led to it in the first place. Could it not be that what we hear in the suffix *-age* (from *paysage*), which seems so neutral and settled, is the collectiveness of *composition*—the passive "assemblage" produced by the vision of an acting subject ("observer")? Could we not hear in it a more operative meaning (of "action" and "result of action"), one that would thenceforth deal with landscape as such and proceed from an effect that landscape itself produces? I wonder, that is,

---

1. "*Si tel assemblage d'arbres, de montagnes, d'eaux et de maisons que nous appelons paysage . . .*" In *Curiosités esthétiques: Salon de 1859*. [Translator's note.]
2. Françoise Chenet-Faugeras, "*Le Paysage comme parti pris*," in *La Théorie du paysage en France, 1974–1994*, ed. Alain Roger (Seyssel, France: Champ Vallon, 1995), 275.

whether the term doesn't spill over the confines of its definition once we indulge ourselves by delving into its potential.

I therefore suggest that what gives rise to landscape is not merely the product of a vision, and thus not a projection of the mind through said vision. I contend that there exists a *landscape effect*—or "landscape-ment," that draws *landscape* from *land* and promotes the former from the latter. The principle has less to do with "structuring," as has often been said (most ably by Augustin Berque, who never veers from the logic of composition), than, as I have begun to say, with *intensification*. There is landscape when "land" is set in tension; when its various elements begin interacting and enter into polarity; and when a manifest increase in intensity results. Just as we acknowledge an "effect of the moment," which engenders an intensification over the monotonous course of time and precipitates the duration (as when we say a "good time"), there exists an effect that qualifies as *landscape-ment*. By producing an intensification in the somber expanse of space, landscape-ment both gathers the expanse into itself and draws forth its *import* [*portée*]. It is with landscape-ment that our vitality connects.

2

"Tension," I admit, is not considered a philosophical concept. Is it perhaps too elementary a notion. Do we therefore relegate it to technical, physical, and physiological spheres, aware of no further meaning in play, and expecting to get no further use out of it? Because we grant it neither ontological vocation, in the great face-off between Being and becoming (as we have done with "potential," *dunamis*, versus "act"), nor ethical vocation, from the point of view of action (that to which the singularization of a virtue or faculty leads), *tension* enters into no construction of the mind. In sum, the notion would seem to be too rife with pure phenomenality for us to steer it toward some purpose (for us to find it some theoretical end) and make it a point of departure—a topic of debate—for thought.

Yet beneath all the axiological overlaps that pile up over centuries and cultures, as we proceed from one ideological construction to the next, there remains the tenacious concept of "living": whenever tension ceases death follows. It is because of tension-setting, because a thing is *under* tension, that something happens, occurs, comes out of inertia, exerts an effect, and can begin to operate and bring about advent. Even now, as I write, there must be a (semantic, rhetorical, and above all notional) tension-setting for the text to begin to "hold up," for an "effect of consciousness" (*Bewusstseinseffekt*, as Freud used to call it) to begin to occur, for there to be an incitement to thought, and for a sentence to stir from its apathy—for it to form a "page." Sentence construction, or correct "composition," is not enough. And the same goes for landscape.

Whenever I look at the mountain head on from my window (Lord knows we have spent hours contemplating it), I find the following: that if not for the modest sheep farm, and especially its acre of grapevine and smattering of cypress trees on the opposite slope, if not for the occasional flat spot, in the incline's hollow, the landscape would greatly suffer. It would lose intensity. Indeed, truth be told, it would cease to be a landscape at all. It would remain "land." Its resource would have run dry. It would drown in itself, fold into its own mass. That happy, simple, discreet reminder of Provençal nature sets the vegetation's ovine opacity in tension. But this is no mere counterpoint, no single element responding to another, and no reciprocal conferring of value. Through the sheep farm the whole mountain soars and finds its fulcrum. The result of this little hollow is that the mountain *tenses up*. Because of the hollow the mountain does not get lost in its spread, does not bog down in itself. An interaction is triggered. It is animated by a *clearing-out and opening-up* [*dégagement*]. Here *animate* is strictly metaphorical, for we, through our "connection" with it, draw from the resulting vitality.

As we might suspect, Chinese thought has leant itself to elucidating this tension through its very mode of operation: opposition-correlation. Shitao, one of the tradition's greatest eighteenth-century thinkers, did more than establish landscape, "mountain(s)/water(s)," as the "form-tension of Heaven and Earth" (形势). He also laid out the resulting tensional network in its diversity:[3]

> Wind and rain, like darkness and light, are the phenomenal manifestation of landscape's breath-energy;
> dispersion and concentration, depth and distance, are landscape's schematic organization;
> the vertical and the horizontal, hollow and relief, constitute landscape's rhythm;
> the side in light and the side in shadow, the pale and the dark, form landscape's condensation of spirit;
> waters and clouds, gathering and dispersal, are landscape's bond;
> foldings and juttings, facing off or turning their respective backs, mark landscape's advance and retreat.

What "gives rise to landscape," then, is the system by which it sets up multiple intersecting and overlapping tensions. Everything in landscape reduces to and converges on that principle. It falls to landscape, as it

---

3. Shitao, *Shan chuan*.

emerges from the flatness of the "land," to focus and concentrate a tension that in the world is ordinarily dispersed.

We can in any case conclude that landscape's effect is not, as has often been claimed, a matter of "harmony" alone. Harmony reflects an "assemblage" born of accord and adaptation. It blurs over *divides* instead of putting them to work (except in the great Heraclitus). Nor is harmony due to an underlying geometry that rationalizes the physical manifestation's structure. On this point Nietzsche is astonishingly Platonic, and mistaken: "I notice that all landscapes which please me permanently have a simple geometrical scheme of lines underneath all their complexity. Without such a mathematical substratum no scenery becomes artistically pleasing" ("The Wanderer and His Shadow," §115).[4] Why in dealing with landscape should we reestablish a (mathematical-metaphysical) layer "underneath" the world that would disqualify the immediacy of living and the sensible? Why, that is, should we do something that Nietzsche otherwise so strenuously denounced? Why does he now serve up the platitude of Platonism? No doubt because both harmony and geometry, proceeding hand in hand, still and forever relate to the logic of *composition*—to the integration of parts into a whole—in keeping with one of European thought's oldest choices. Landscape, however, deals not with *integration* but with *intensification*. It meets the demands not of *order* but of *activation*. Landscape withers and vanishes—loses tension—if what we perceive in it is figures and schemes, models of the ideal, and if we think of it as a garden.

3

This notional divide, advancing gradually along the lines of my dissidence, is a breach that will never close. To one side, I can consider that landscape issues from my own vision-conception: in other words, from my own capacity to fashion it into "landscape." Here the landscape is the fruit of a production—an "artialization," as they say[5]—that I undertake in line with my own schemas. The (detrimental) consequence is a landscape "of biases" (Françoise Chenet-Faugeras). We thus christen the "landscape" "with a whole series of aesthetic, commercial, and even ideological values: this 'assemblage' rather than that." In short, all "land" can become "landscape"; it is all eligible for the title. I need only adjust my eye accordingly. A landscape has less intrinsic value than what it gains culturally.

---

4. From Paul V. Cohn's translation of *Human, All Too Human: A Book for Free Spirits* (New York: MacMillan, 1913). [Translator's note.]

5. "They" are those who echo philosopher Alain Roger, who borrowed Montaigne's neologism for his *Court traité du paysage* (Paris: Gallimard, 1997). [Translator's note.]

To the other side of the divide, I can consider that landscape, rather than being a construction of my perception, stems from an intrinsic effect, one produced directly within the world, within the "mountains" and "waters" (the solid and the shifting, the apparent and the rustling, and so on). Here landscape arises because the "land" is set into tension, or intensified. Land's promotion to landscape thus lies *within the landscape*—or, rather, exists through it, in the *interspace*. Polarities arise—or, better yet, enter into "activity"—and become more marked, and more diverse. Their play becomes operative. There arises a *tensional field*, whose first result is that landscape becomes a matter less of the "view" than of *living*.

We ascribe to the first hypothesis everything we know about landscape's cultural invention in Europe, namely, that it has steadily conquered new ground even as the norms of our appreciation have shifted. Alain Roger reminds us correctly that "landscape" was at first limited to the countryside, fields, and bucolic subjects and that before the eighteenth century mountain country, with its chaotic heaps, was still "dreadful" (Montesquieu crossing the Tyrol) and the sea, cursed by the deluge, was fit only to inspire fear and offered nothing to look at. For these landscapes to appear—that is, for us to acknowledge them—we needed to dissolve the prejudices that crippled our sight, to shed the many blinders from our eyes. We needed Haller to write his great poem on the Alps, for instance, and Rousseau to lodge his lovers in their midst. Only then, at last, could sterile, unwholesome mountain country pique the interest of tourists and travelers with its "picturesque" quality. Indeed, we needed nothing less than to promote the "sublime" above the "beautiful," affixing our seal to the oxymoron and raising it above rhetorical flourish. We could thus invoke and legitimize a fertile contradiction to liberate the perpetual harmony. With the "repulsive" being revealed as "attractive," and "horror" blending with the "exquisite," the ocean could aspire to be more than a terrifying expanse where we feared to venture; it could become the expanse where we discovered immensity.

Since then we have never stopped educating our eye and pushing the envelope: undoing our learned notion of landscape, denouncing its conventions. We have incorporated forest, marsh, and desert. After all, isn't everything "landscape-able"? They say we need only adapt our cultural habitus to modernity before we start seeing landscape everywhere: landscape worthy of "contemplation." Indeed, the greatest potential for landscape lies precisely in the most recalcitrant land: the land most difficult to admire at first blush. We are called to this effort not only by the new vistas that science has opened to our inspection, and that might harbor even greater beauty than our usual view (the ocean floor, say, or the earth as seen from another planet), but also by wastelands, no-man's-lands,[6] suburbs, dumps, highway interchanges, and devastated fields—things that bourgeois aesthetics has long resisted and to which art (highly instructive in this regard) has now turned. Gone are the days of the postcard landscape touched by the gods. Now, wherever my eye may alight, my perception must undertake its own reeducation. And this is all to the good. The mold is broken, and truth comes once again to light.

4

This position is at present, I admit, hardly assailable because in general agreement with the current ideology (the much-lauded abrogation of boundaries). But can we leave it at that? For we note (with Alain Roger) that painters, though formerly helping things along and though spurring us to keep pushing the cultural envelope of landscape and extend the sphere of aesthetics to the whole world and thus to all "land," have themselves renounced the landscape-ment of mountain country. Why? Is this anodyne? It is indeed the case after all that painting came to a halt midslope and has climbed no further, as if painters had refused further ascent. "The higher one goes, the less the scenes lend themselves to painterly depiction."[7] It is photography, coming along at just the right time, that has taken the torch from painting. "The failure seems definitive, and marks a significant event in the history of art." The event is all the more significant because it was with painting—indeed, *in* painting, through its Renaissance shift—that landscape was invented in Europe. So why has painting gone no further in conquering the summits? From the look of things, it is not as if painting (and by the same token landscape) were content only with the mean, or feared the extraordinary and the trials of pushing the limits. But why, then? Could there not be a faint demarcation here, a signal, however discreet, that the pictorial and landscape are incompatible with *endless aesthetization*? By spotting this fissure, peering from this angle, tugging on this thread, we cannot help but observe once again that we have yet to uncover what actually "gives rise to landscape."

Returning to the previous distinction, then, I wonder whether a panorama of snow-capped peaks visible from a mountain pass, or the vastness of the sea or sky, does not constitute, in its immaculate power, an extreme, astonishingly beautiful *view*—a view of breathtaking, un-

---

6. The term appears in English in the original French text. [Translator's note.]
7. Roger, *Court traité du paysage*, 95.

dreamed-of beauty—but still not a landscape. According to Altmann (quoted by Alain Roger), "one of the most beautiful spectacles imaginable in nature is a sea of ice. . . . It is a sight of marvelous beauty." So there is "sight [*coup d'œil*]," "beauty," and even an attainment of the "sublime," but what then? The summit of Azpiglia photographed head on (by Aimé Civiale) is like Notre Dame de Paris contemplated from behind the apse. There is a *monopolizing* view; the eye is fixed and can no longer wander here and there; things are reduced to the absolute. The eye is conquered, pure "spectacle" indeed. It is "spectacular," as we are wont to say. We formerly did not know how to look at the open sea or mountain peaks as *spectacula* (in the sense that the Seven Wonders of the World are *omnium terrarum spectacula*). Faced with such wonders we can only fix our gaze, hold it in suspension, stare in a stupor, and halt.

The open sea or a mountain summit is a landscape run dry; the landscape in them has ebbed away. It is not merely because we positively perceive, qualify, and poeticize what comes into view that landscape arises. The shore, not the open sea, is landscape; the mountain, not its summit, is landscape—not so much because I do not wish to (cannot) live in (dwell in) these places but because they lack the intensification. It is eminently diverse, abounding, operating by variation, and weaving its network, to which living can connect. The shore, with its coast of capes and bays, its vegetation, its houses, and its islands, is landscape. There would be no "Gulf of Naples" without Capri. The shore is endlessly setting up tensions, opposing and correlating land and sea, high and low, finite and infinite, the vegetal and the water, the varied and the slack, the inhabited and the uninhabitable, and so on. The open sea is but a marine element that contrasts unilaterally with its opposite number, the sky, or else subtly blends with it. Our *sight* is captivated by that unique tension.

The mountain summit, in like manner, is but ice and height. Everywhere. There the tension of high and low, or of the rocky and the grassy, the wooded and the arid, the tufted and the barren, the sinuous and the jagged, and the misted and the chiseled, slackens. And, to begin with, we have no further sense of a mountain stretching up from its solid base and standing erect. We lose the *compossibility* that established the breadth of the "mountain" in the eyes of China's painters. When nature goes to extremes, becomes radical, or indeed monopolizes itself, we begin to perceive everywhere the same, equal and generalized intensity, but we no longer feel the *intensification*. We no longer feel the tension set in, or *rise*. Once lavished—in successive planes, allowing the eye to proceed from near to far—this tension makes the "whole" into a world. By means of a silent *clearing-out and opening-up* [*dégagement*], it extracts from "land" a "landscape."

5

A certain term was coined after the Second World War, that apogee of destructive power. We know its birthdate in French (1964), some four centuries after that of *paysage* (*landscape*), because it too met what had become a patent need and call for change. This time it came not from the Dutch painters but from the American conservation movement. The term was *environment*, and it took up what the notion of landscape, associated exclusively with vision and considered strictly from the aestheticizing standpoint, had relinquished. *Environment* is the substitute term—no longer artistic, alas, but technocratic—born not of happy invention (the "subject" sweeping his sovereign eye over the world) but of repair (we must save the planet from the excessive change wrought by the Subject's sovereignty). This term clearly has served to reconnect landscape to *living*. But have we truly laid bare the transfer? After all, *environment* has filled the void that *landscape*, with its restriction to the visual and its exclusive focus on "beauty," had surreptitiously hollowed out in our relation to the world.

Because it designates all of the conditions—natural, physical, chemical, and biological, as well as cultural and social—likely to affect living organisms and human activity, the word *environment* sets man squarely in the landscape as an inhabitant. Man is thus no longer a mere passing "observer." *Environment* speaks, moreover, to the diffuse influence of the "milieu" (the "environs")—not just on conscious subjects but, indeed, on all living beings: precisely because they *are alive*. The "environment" has prompted a discreet but major shift in contemporary ideology. At first associated with social concerns, politics, and protest movements, in time the notion took on an administrative bent, becoming a matter of policy and implementation. But we mustn't allow this to camouflage the theoretical revolution it represents.

An "environment," first of all, is no longer limited by a "defining" horizon (as in the Greek *horizein*, ὁρίζειν) or by any cutting out that an eye effects relative to its position. The bounds of such "environs" remain forever and inevitably vague. The milieu and the surroundings can have no marked boundary. Moreover, the relation in question is no longer made up of active perception, of an initiative-wielding self, but of influence passively felt by an organism of infinite diversity, and of continual exchanges that for the most part escape our attention. The notion of environment has sidled up to and dethroned the notion of landscape, though without proclamation. It has also inverted landscape's assumptions, or at least those that triumphant classical reason had laid down: namely, the subject's autonomy and power of determination. By signifying a disengagement from the insular, knowing, desiring *ego*—from the builder of the perceptual constructions on which European landscape-thought rests—environment has given voice to what landscape had suppressed: not just the indeterminable imbuing of the *invasive* (as the inverse and complement to the *evasive*) but also, and to a greater extent, the inseparability of the living from its "element."

It is understandable, then, that the partisans of a purely aesthetic ("artializing") conception of landscape should denounce any conflation of environment and landscape, and indeed any hint of contamination between the two notions: that is, any tainting of landscape by environment. It is understandable that they should frown upon any contact between ecological concerns and artistic pleasure. Let us keep the two orders of things free of mutual interference, hermetically separate. (This, of course, is the position notably of Alain Roger.) But I cannot help seeing this insistent segregation as symptomatic of the suppression accomplished by our European definition of landscape, whose consequence we can gauge in the following, logically consistent distinction of principle: on the one hand, we have the landscape "as it lies," *in situ*, and remark that we are causing its deterioration day after day with our technical means; on the other hand, we have at the same time the landscape "of our perception," *in visu*, a perception that we can always transform, educate, or reverse by changing our perceptual schemas—such that we can always re-aestheticize what intrudes upon and disturbs our conventional vision. That said, however, could we rest easy given the *fault* that this cleavage reveals between landscape and *living*? Would making a *cut* (as in the customary gesture of metaphysics) once again be our only way out?

Henceforth the question is no longer whether I can aestheticize, artialize, or poeticize everything that I see but whether everything that my perception qualifies in those terms gives rise to "landscape." We long ago brought within the scope of art the previously unrecognized power of the dilapidated, the abandoned, the undone, and the forsaken—in short, everything that smacks of defeat and dereliction. This rehabilitation follows logically from our general championing of the negative, which informs so much of our modernity. Since at least Romanticism, moreover, we have known how fertile it is to aestheticize the ugly in revolt against normative taste and harmony. The ugly is less amenable to established taste and convention, and wakes Beauty from its torpor. It is, in fact, more rewarding, because it is more trouble to extract its quality. Still, what prevents me from promoting ugliness, reworked in my mind, into landscape (as when one takes the train from Paris to Roissy[8])? It is not the occasional wretchedness of the area, for that would only provide further material to

---

8. That is, to Charles de Gaulle airport, located outside the town of Roissy. [Translator's note.]

aestheticize. Nor can it be the lack of order, regularity, symmetry, or any such thing, because elsewhere we find neighborhoods of well-laid-out, well-aligned, orderly houses, with lawns and broad perspectives, all resulting from urban planning, that tend to seem just as unlivable—just as *un-landscape-able*, if not more so.

6

There, irredeemably, we will find nothing but "land." Unless polarities emerge, intensities develop here and there, differentials fall into order, and factors subsequently activate among themselves there is no landscape. All remains slack—or, let us say, atonic. The various components remain as they are, insofar as they are, such as they are, folded in on themselves, and unresponsive to one another. They do not enter into tension. Because they do not activate one another they cannot mobilize a "subject," even a "reflective" one. The place remains somber or, once again, "atonic," and there can be no such thing as an atonic landscape. Sad, perhaps (depending on my mood), but not depressed. Landscape, disengaging from "land," is *intensive*. Its negation is *atony*, the absence of life-generating tension.

The underdeveloped Greek concept, then, is *tonos*: underdeveloped because kept under the reign of *kallos*, τὸ κάλλος, "beauty." To elucidate landscape we must seek it out, sift through what metaphysics has left in the shadows. With sovereign authority, the Beautiful has dominated Western thought (with a Platonism that will not be undone), because in beauty and in beauty alone gleams the intelligible, because beauty has opened a breach in the sensible through which we glimpse our desired ideality. But in promoting *kallos* and rendering its power absolute, to make it a path to salvation, we have relegated *tonos* (τόνος), its discreet rival, to manual, material, and technical uses, to disdained and disparate uses. It designates the one reality as well as the other, because all are equally prone to "tension": a ligament, a strap, the twisted string of a net, the rigging of a machine, and the tendons and muscles of the human body. It denotes in Greek the "tension" in the strings of a lyre as well as the sinews of the soul, breath, and effort, of the voice and sentiment, of a sentence's style and a verse's rhythm, and of the tonic accent in a language.

There in the darkness, apart from the elucidating daylight of metaphysics, in the *tonos* of the tonal and the tonic, all things that pertain to *the interior*, at whatever level of phenomenality, are interlinked; something stretches out, deploys, and is triggered; an effect breaks free. In short, activity or operativity becomes possible. It is precisely here that causal explanation—the explanation of the external agent, the great wellspring of Greek intelligence—fizzles out. It is here that the (sudden) generalizing light of transcendence (the light that in the destiny of Greek philosophy starts to establish the status of the "Idea" whose prototype is beauty) has no grounds to intervene. Thus the term *tension* remained specifically (locally) descriptive, Plutarchian rather than Platonic in its intelligence, and was never, despite widespread use, built up into a concept. At bottom this concept would have been physical (the "tension" of a spring) and no longer metaphysical, Beauty henceforth demanding *eros* as source of attraction. After all, if one did not think through internal tension, one would have to invoke Eros to ensure the relation: it is Love, as great mediator, of the exterior that "elevates" us to Beauty.

But landscape's peculiarity is that it removes us from the metaphysical construction hammered out by ideality, by both Beauty and aroused Love. One does not idealize a landscape, unless by lapsing into symbolism (although symbolism kills landscape). But there is *effectively* landscape insofar as world-stuff rises up in *tonos* to that condition: insofar as world-stuff is set in tension variously, on its own and by immanence; or insofar as the land "tonifies" in it. If we then exclaim, in a resultative (qualitative) way, that a landscape is "beautiful," if we affix the qualifier to the landscape like a label, it is doubtless because we are confining it to the visual, for otherwise we would have to take pains to think through a *physics of life*, and burst the bounds of the concept. Landscape is an ample manifestation of this.

7

From this angle we can make yet another distinction between *landscape* and *garden*. The two stand in opposition insofar as the garden evokes the interior and the bounded, promoting intimacy and habitation, and landscape pertains to the outside, calling for travel; in landscape we are but passing through. It is nonetheless customary to consider the garden as a condensation of landscape: as landscape's reinforced "artialization." The two are linked, moreover, by the same, privileged relation to painting—*ut pictora hortus*. I myself am not convinced, first of all, that the distinction between the interior and the exterior is all that valid. (I prefer to distinguish the *closed* from the *open*; we will return to this.) I am not convinced that the distinction does not yet again, as ever, restrict landscape to visual perception and thus to the mere attribute of separation and distance. Nor am I certain that in "contemplating" a landscape from afar we do not also, secretly, dream of dwelling in said landscape ("that house, yonder . . ."), instead of being content to traverse it. We also *bind* ourselves to landscape.

Thus the distinction to be made, if any, is between the two kinds of garden. Their opposition is customary but bears consideration, because exemplary and illustrative. Mere mention of it here will serve as verification. On the one hand, the so-called French garden is, in effect, a construction of my perception, favoring the viewpoint and the panorama. It is there chiefly to be *looked at*, the sovereign eye of a Subject imposing its order on nature. ("A garden," remarks Saint-Simon about Versailles, "is the superb pleasure of forcing nature's hand.") By its geometry, moreover, the French garden is manifestly disjunct from "land," and through its modeling it is in like manner detached from landscape. Parallelism in particular, as a law of depiction, lends it the order of an abstraction, which runs contrary to tension-setting polarity.

On the other hand (perhaps at the antipode?), we have the Chinese garden, whose primary function is to restore one's energy. It offers no alignments or perspectives where the admiring eye can relish *compositional* balance and symmetry. Nor does it offer broad alleys where, at best, one can "get some air" and take a stroll. Instead, it *tenses up* processually, like a dragon's body, in the most various alternations: the empty and the full, the sinuous (down to the bridges) and the straight, the rocky and the vegetal, the aquatic and the mineral, the raised and the steep, the shadowy and the bright, and so forth. In short, it repeats and condenses the great correlation of "mountains and waters." The Chinese garden introduces no transcendent order of reason. It concentrates landscape, like a "world in miniature" (as in R. Alfred Stein's lovely title[9]), with a maximum of polarities. By "wandering" at leisure from one to another (*you*, 游)—or, rather, *between*[10] them—we reactivate its vital tension. Because it varies so densely between these opposites, the Chinese garden arranges itself as a continual respiration, provides egress from atony, and "feeds" life.

8

Why, inversely, does *living* find itself imperiled if there is a dearth of or break in landscape? Consider an electric line crossing the landscape we used to look at from the high window of our favorite house, set amid olive trees. (We peer out from a decrepit room with a rickety floor, a room we have expressly reserved.) Why should we long for the ability to wave a hand and erase that cable? Why should that line "hurt" us so? Why should it make it so hard—no use denying it—for us to "live"? Why de-

---

9. The full title is *Le Monde en petit: jardins en miniatures et habitations dans la pensée réligieuse d'Extreme-Orient*. [Translator's note.]

10. Jullien's use of the word *between* (*entre*) is a reference to his concept of the *interspace* (*l'entre*), developed in chapter 7. [Translator's note.]

spite all our closely reasoned arguments should it ruin everything? More than just "hurt our eyes," as we say, it constrains, squeezes, cleaves in twain all the soaring around it, and does so all by itself. Otherwise, what else could lie at the root of our suffering? Is our "suffering" strictly mental? (Does it not strike at our "vitality" as well?) The trouble is not that the electric line, with its tall pylon, belongs to another era, or has chosen the wrong setting to remind us of modern industry and its economic ravages in what would otherwise be a perfectly Renaissance decor. The trouble is that the line is exerting its effect all by itself. It is linked to nothing else anywhere in the landscape, to nothing in the "whole" that it chips away at. It *enters into tension* with nothing. Within the landscape it is, rather than an additional element of variation, a disfiguring intrusion.

Those who maintain that landscape is, at best, the product of an artialization by the educated eye have an easy time mocking the constant griping over what we have come to call "eyesores." We have all seen these things, said to "spoil" (an obviously suspect term) a village or a field. An eyesore might be a pylon, a transformer, or a shed. Worse, it might be a "Maison Phénix,"[11] plonked down and ringed with a rectilinear fence. Or else it might be an alignment of numberless, petunia-bearing cement planters in the tiny old village square. Learn to see the aesthetics of abrupt verticality, we are told. Learn to appreciate trenchant linearity. Embrace the geometry. These forms too have been invented. Stop seeing these things as additions, and start seeing them as new components. Unlearn your ideal landscape, your learned (settled) landscape. Forget Corot. Not "Get used to it (after a while you won't see it anymore)." But instead "Integrate it into your perception. Use it to build from scratch what in this land gives rise to 'landscape.'"

I myself am not so sure that we can so easily rid ourselves of this question; that the foregoing plea, while intelligent, is enough. While these contemporary productions do seem to have their own aesthetic, which blends into and stirs the past, we know too, with a knowledge quietly gained through experiment, that in landscape it is not the "thing in itself" that counts. What makes an eyesore an eyesore—to continue the metaphor—is not the offending "thing." A pylon is not ugly but majestic in structure, and a wind turbine is elegant. We have an "eyesore," however, when the thing in question breaks the *tensional field* in the landscape's weave, when the thing interrupts or pokes a hole in the landscape, causing the landscape to hemorrhage intensity, as it were.

We know very well that a forest of electrical wires, like a knot of highways, can form a landscape. Activity, work, and density and its din, set-

---

11. Trade name in France for a kind of inexpensive house. [Translator's note.]

ting their multiple tensions, also generate landscape—indeed, do it better than bucolic sheep farms. Elements offend when they lack the intrinsic consistency to serve as poles in a polarity. They do not so much fail to enter into *composition* (to "integrate," or to meet the old rigors of harmony) as fail to enter into *correlation* in, or with, the existing landscape. They cannot cooperate with it. But let tensions be set up, let a new circuit be closed, and they too will become factors and vectors of landscape-ment. Because the trouble is not with "contemporaneity" and its inability to blend in, we should be able to understand that neither is it a matter of "safeguarding." Across the lagoon from Venice, the petro-Manhattan of Mestre, with its bristling pylons and pipes, also gives rise to landscape.

On the banks of the Seine at the eastern end of the Marais I always felt, or *experienced*, a wrenching of the heart on seeing the Sully-Morland office building standing there as proud as can be. With its two outstretched arms and functional, somewhat Soviet structure, the building was not exactly "ugly," nor did its sixties Modernism blend poorly with the more classical buildings around it. But the building was lying there like an island, "plonked down," encumbering but inconsistent, and insufficiently detached to form a pole (not in the clear like the Eiffel Tower or Beaubourg[12]) and thus *entering into tension* with nothing. Then, one fine day, three similar little buildings sprung up, side by side, radicalizing the flattened Sully-Morland roof and refining its line. The new buildings suddenly gave rise to a correlation. Between them they spread a new net, superimposing it on Paris—and in so doing took a stump to the "eyesore," as it were, and shaded it off.

We can draw a similar lesson, though in reverse, from what France, by metaphor, has come to call *mitage* [literally, moth-eating]. (And why resort to metaphor if not because of our primordial lack of a concept that would need to question?) The term was coined by landscapers and environmental professionals in response to a new threat to landscape-ment. Like holes in a moth-eaten cloth, structures are appearing gradually and sporadically in the landscape. On the one hand, the "eyesore"—or *verrue* [worm], as they call it—opens a breach in the tensional field, the snag causing a sudden drop in intensity. On the other, *mitage* is the swarming of new buildings such that tension-setting no longer advenes. Old villages cluster their dwellings around the church or the lordly manor. We see them raise the tension by deepening the divide with the surrounding wilderness. From this a landscape takes flight and soars. When villages let in a few large trees the interaction only grows stronger; as the Chinese say, a spot of yin activates the yang. *Mitage*, however, scatters the struc-

---

12. The other name for the Centre Pompidou. [Translator's note.]

tures (each house having its gate, its cedar hedgerow, and its little patch of land) and thus fails to create enough density for correlation. In other words, there is too little concentration of the *one* for the *other* to emerge. Tension disintegrates, and polarity falls to pieces. Landscape's effect dissolves, and its *soaring* is lost.

VII

✢

Singularization, Variation, Remove

1

The intensification that promotes land into landscape demands some unfolding.[1] At least three factors coordinate to effect this promotion. (Might we conceive of a *landscape system*?) Landscape proceeds first from a *singularization*, which brings the landscape to my attention. As I drive along I am suddenly no longer willing to pass things by, no longer content to continue on my way. I want to stop things from racing past, and therefore come to a halt. But is this a matter of "attention" only? The instance of singularity emphasizes what is unique in a landscape, what is to be found nowhere else. Suddenly, with a certainty that brooks no doubt, we know we will not find this instance anywhere else. Singularity causes the landscape to emerge from the anonymity and inertness of things. More than just detach the landscape from the flatness of a monotonous and endless expanse, it makes the landscape salient. It "awakens" the landscape by bringing out the landscape's individuation, brushing off the dust that has settled upon it in the continuum of places and days. I have a sense of being suddenly and effectively there, *da-sein*—in a "there" that sticks out—and thus of *existing* myself.

---

1. Here as elsewhere in the book the meaning of Jullien's special verb *unfold* (*déplier*) approximates the meaning of the more idiomatic English verb *unpack*, in the sense of extracting information from some sort of intellectual packet. I have opted to use *unfold* in this special sense because it reverses Jullien's fundamental image of the fold as a sort of accordion file of thought. A closed (or folded) "file" keeps information unavailable to us. Jullien's philosophy is meant to be an unfolding of, or a retrieval of lost assumptions in, our thought. [Translator's note.]

But landscape's singularization is itself a result. A landscape enters into tension (sets up tension) by deepening the divide not merely with the surrounding "land," from which it singularizes, but primarily within itself, or in its *interspace*. Such is the internal *variation* that condenses landscape's polarity, and from that polarity condenses potentiality, and then produces activation: the vector for *vitality*. The alternation not only creates respiration but also leads to renewal. For "living" (through variation) and "existing" (through singularization), landscape accomplishes both simultaneously. We must learn to distinguish and link the two.

Another vector for landscape is the *remove* that landscape opens up, deploying "beyond-ness" but doing so within this world, by effacement and shading. Remove thus contributes to landscape's aura. It takes landscape's traits and opens them up beyond their limited character, rendering them evasive. They become factors in a vague, nameless going-beyond, and thus give rise to aspiration. Might not this overflowing, this transformation into the other, be itself something peculiar to life in terms of life's becoming? At any rate, I believe that this trinomial lays out conditions that all landscape must meet. These same three conditions, moreover, prevent landscape from being a matter of some subjective—some will say cultural—artialization. They require landscape to proceed from an effect peculiar to landscape itself (or that belongs to it in particular), and thanks to which landscape actually qualifies as a *resource*.

2

By our current standard, there is landscape first and foremost when singularity is attained within it, but what does "singularity" mean here? The singular is not, for instance, the extreme. As we already know, an extreme view (of desert, sea, mountains, etc.) does not by itself amount to landscape. Neither does the extraordinary. A landscape does not owe its value to the rarity of its features. There is landscape, rather, when the individuation within is sufficiently acute to specify the landscape. What is *peculiar* to it appears. And yet a landscape's singularity is not "what sets it apart" or its particularity, which again is what distinguishes a landscape from a "view." As I suggested at the start, a view is always a "view of," a "view toward," adhering to its location. A landscape, meanwhile, transcends within itself its locality such that the locality conveys an entire world. Even while being "a" landscape, separate from all others, it is a "whole"—the world. In other words, there is no landscape unless the place exists as (amounts to) a world. There is no landscape unless what gives rise to "world-ness" opens a crack, deploys, is revealed in the landscape's particularity.

Bringing to bear the (still effective) Hegelian machine, we might say that the "particularity" (of this or that "view": *das Besondere*), having withdrawn from the "common" (*gemein*), remains stuck in its partiality and folds back into it; whereas there is landscape when particularity, while going beyond itself through *singularity* (*das Einzelne*), simultaneously promotes itself into a "universal" of nature, of all nature, although thereby becoming *effective*. To say, as we have already said, that a landscape is never a "corner" of the world, that it comes to constitute landscape insofar as it contains a whole, insofar as it contains all manner of things, within its unicity (as Chinese so aptly signifies in "mountains and waters," or "wind/light"), is already to acknowledge the vocation of the Singular. However, the "singularity" of landscape—like the "moment" when the determinateness of the "land," through its particularity, brings forth the "all-things-in-common-ness" (*allgemein*) of what gives rise to world-ness—is precisely what, by individuation, causes the character of *existing* to come forth, to emerge.

For we know, the scholastics having elaborated on Aristotle, that existence is "proper to the singular": *existentia est singularium*. The only form of existence, in other words, is singular existence, of the "each" category (*kath'hekaston*), as opposed to the generality on which the discourse of science rests. In still other words, *only the singular exists*. (As Aristotle, Socrates, and Callias used to say, we cure this man here, not "man" in general.) Singularization, then, is what *makes existence emerge*, what brings things *into existence*. This is why singularization is to be demanded. The demand for the Singular culminates in Christianity, which, through Kierkegaard, gives birth to "existentialism." (Whatever people might say, are Hegel and Kierkegaard really so far apart on this point?) This is what gives life to a landscape. Landscape is "land" that, by singularization, expresses (renders sensible) what "existing" (in its unicity) effectively is. The *fact* of landscape is to bring existence physically to the surface, before consciousness, by virtue strictly of the individuation that detaches it from the repetitiveness, banality, or "generality" (monotony) of the "land."

By the same token, in return, by *intimate* echo, when we encounter a landscape, when we enter into that emerging singularity (for we "encounter" a landscape as we would encounter an "Other," detaching him from anonymous "others"), we feel ourselves to be singular beings. We feel ourselves to exist in an "effective," and no longer commonplace, sense. (Our sense of existence is no longer slumberous, no longer slips the mind.) We feel ourselves *ex-isting* in and through landscape insofar as the landscape leads us to emerge reactively from the flat continuity of "land," from a continuity that tends to slip from consciousness. Better yet, let us say that landscape compels us to feel its existence proportionally to its singularization and thus brings out our own individual existence, or brings us back to our own sense of existence. Landscape poetry (as with Xie Lingyun) is the ordinary playing out of this logic. It leads us from the evocation of a landscape's singularity to a subject's meditation as he reconsiders his own life. This does not mean that landscape is a convenient, docile object, always at hand for conventional subjectivation, or the medium for facile projection, as Romanticism too often made it out to be. Rather, it restores me in my existence as a subject when I encounter it, here and now, individually. It conjures that existence for me.

3

It should come as no surprise that we should evoke a landscape less by "describing" it, with an endless and pointless inventory of characteristics, than by bringing out its singularity in what we say. China, which fears nothing so much as burying its sense of existence beneath abstraction, has delighted in setting up systems of oppositions, a typology, through which to elicit the singular. If the southeastern mountains are grandiose and eminent, says Guo Xi,[2] it is not "that Heaven and Earth have favored them" but that the land there is very low, plain, and bare, and the ground thin and shallow. The mountains thus rise to steep summits and abrupt cliffs, with waterfalls of vertiginous height. They thus stand in perfect contrast to the lavish and massive northwestern mountains, where the soil is very thick and the waters carve sinuous gorges. These mountains run without a break for thousands of *li*.[3] Nor is it "that Heaven and Earth have been partial to these," continues Guo Xi. Instead, they *stand out as singular*.

For hours as we follow the coast of, say, Languedoc (or the Adriatic) I will perceive nothing that *stands out as singular*, or at least nothing singular enough to bring out *peculiarity* or landscape (nothing worth a journey). Land and sea go by, border on each other, lie juxtaposed, and scarcely touch but never break the monotonous thread. Tension never sets in; the unique never bursts forth. In the chain of events we lose our sense of existing; it dozes off. For landscape to arise—for us to feel a sense of "being there," as effective *Dasein*—the sea must rush into the land and swirl, the mountain must precipitously jut, and rockiness must oppose the smooth, fragmentary slack of the expanse. Above all, unevenness must develop; some "relief" (a lucid term) must cut across the endless horizontality. Who has not scanned vast stretches from a train or a car, eager for the saving grace of such singularization? The painters were not mistaken to

---

2. Guo Xi, "Shan shui xun," in *Lingquan gaozhi*, in *Hualun Congkan*, ed. Yu Anlan (Beijing: Zhonggua shuju, 1977), 20.

3. The traditional Chinese mile, about a third as long as the English mile. [Translator's note.]

apply their rusty colors to the two coastal extremities of Collioure and L'Estaque. But these landscapes, as we can see, as we can *live*, have since been definitively erased.

The singularization that qualifies a landscape occurs through contrast with "land" but also with other landscapes. A landscape can so stand out as singular—can so affirm its peculiarity—as to exclude all others, as if rendering them impossible or stripping them of reality. On the Mediterranean shore I forget all about Brittany. Truth be told, I can hardly even imagine it, or else I imagine it as existing in another world, and myself as living another life. (And Brittany only does itself a disservice when it seeks to renounce its cold alliance of lime, granite, and slate and coat itself in shades of ocher: that is, when it pretends to be "the South of France.") But Brittany and Normandy lie side by side, as if to emphasize the intervening divide and stand out. Indeed, we wonder how we can go from here to there, in our senses or our thought. How can we go from the pleasures of the one to the disquiet of the other? What upheavals in our frame of mind and physical being must we endure to withstand the rupture that occurs here, beneath the apparent continuity of the coast? The one prolongs the other, but *everything* changes—each landscape being a "whole"—and takes pride in the change.

Will we ever be able to account fully for the "whole" of what thus changes, of what gives rise to a landscape's singularity but does so by forming a "whole"? Will we ever manage to ferret it out as we go from one to the other, and not only from chalk to granite, from lime to slate, from undulation to crevice, from the open ("cheerful") to the stern, from the retracted to the set apart, or from the Norman skies of a Eugène Boudin to the great, tormented flatlands of Brittany? In Normandy one is "Impressionist," whereas in Brittany (cf. Sérusier's *Le Talisman*) one is "Primitivist" ("Spiritualist," "Pontavenist"[4]). On one side, sensation is nuanced; on the other, it is radicalized or gutted. Thus one evokes a land when making the starkest contrast with the other, as if singularization made landscape into an essence. Normandy is clement, harmonious, and subdued even when the wind and rain kick up. It is "restful," one will say, talking avowed but somehow needful nonsense. Meanwhile, adjacent Brittany, with its jagged coasts, is extreme. Instead of prairies, we have gorses and the pulsing tide. Brittany is rude to the eye, the ear, and the touch. It is gloomy even at midday. And in fine weather, when it no longer makes you believe in sunken islands and mirages, Brittany is too fine, too blue—and even more mysterious. Brittany is sublime. Normandy is never sublime. Nor is (charming) Provence. Are these images

---

4. Literally, an inhabitant of Pont-Aven, a town in Brittany famous for the many painters who have sojourned there. [Translator's note.]

("postcards") too broad in their strokes, or are these clichés of language in fact too restrained, too discreet? For as soon as we open the door and set foot on a well-worn path we "drink in"—rather than see—the *whole* of the singular.

4

Land becomes landscape also, and more primordially, as an effect of *variation*, not by deepening the divide between it and other land—which amounts to singularization—but by opening a divide within itself, and thus increasing its own tension. Because the effect of landscape is to draw land out of its monotony—or better yet out of its atony—"land" unperturbed by an internal divide has two necessary consequences. Not only do we become indifferent to said land as it goes by, our senses finding nothing to hook into, but also life in said land turns atonic. It gets mired in repetition. It languishes, for lack of further encounters. We get vast plains (or, worse, the American "corn belt") and Brittany from the four-lane highway. Because it cuts through the landscape rather than hugging the relief (bypassing Brittany's valleys), and because it follows a trajectory that crosses out the divides and stands aloof, the rectilinear highway parches the landscape, makes it "run dry." The result is somnolence. It is not so much that there is nothing more to see but that there is nothing more to sketch out an amplitude that vitality might connect with, nothing more to stir vitality. We are warned against "falling asleep at the wheel" on highways, but we fall asleep because there is no landscape to keep us going, to hold us in suspense, and to *activate* us with its variations.

In this era of globalization, under this reign of uniformity, it is good to recall a bit of wisdom come down to us from the dawn of time: to make a world, as everyone from the Stoics to the Church fathers has tirelessly repeated, we need "all manner of things," but this "all" is "all" only if it is "various." This need is what the Greeks called *poikilia* (ποικιλία). Otherwise our world is merely "filled" by repetition, sterile reproduction to the point of saturation. There is completion (*sumplêrôsis*, συμπλήρωσις, in Greek) but no "world" in its beauty through diversity, or *cosmos*. In persistently rehashing theodicy over the millennia to justify the presence of evil in Creation and absolve God, we have shown that every painting needs "shadows" to bring out its colors by contrast. Or, as Descartes put it, the world is all the more perfect for my own imperfection. Through my very faults—that is, by the internal divide that I introduce—I contribute to the world's necessary overall variation.

You cannot make a "world" out of "sameness." You need the one and the other. Better yet, you have the one only through and thanks to the other. This is what "land" promoted to "landscape" through variation brings to light. In landscape *the one* and *the other* are simply juxtaposed, and the juxtaposition is what gives rise to landscape. As Chinese thought, for its part, quickly came to understand, there is "the one" only through "the other" (yin and yang), and it is from the one that the other draws its possibility. In China, then, there is no possible ontology, nothing with which to think the in-itself "with respect to itself" (*kath'hauto*). Instead, there is landscape-thought: the one tautens, emerges, juts forth, and has "relief"—the one, that is, can "be"—only through its other. There is no high (of the mountain) without the low (of the water). The one has no solidity without—except in view of—the other's fluidity. The luminosity of the summits is revealed—set apart—only because it emerges from shadowy valleys.

In dealing with landscape, then, I must return to the same concepts of "divide" and "interspace" with which I have elsewhere deconstructed ontology,[5] and must first distinguish between *divide* and *difference*. Difference merely classifies and specifies by distinction (as in the vast erudition of a naturalist, the erudition that goes into a herbarium). It puts things in order, sets them side by side in accordance with their appearance and properties, and arrives at various kinds of trees, minerals, flowers, and even clouds. A *divide* is a wholly different matter. Rather than a distinction, it introduces a distance. It sets in tension what it has separated. And in so doing opens an *interspace*, but the "interspace" is not a matter of the "in-itself." It is *in*, or *by*, the *interspace* that opens between the high (of the mountain) and the low (of the water)—between the immobile and the shifting, the opaque and the transparent, the manifest and the rustling—that landscape deploys. Properly speaking, then, landscape is, as I have already said, nowhere in particular, because it can nowhere be isolated, can *be assigned to no one place*. Landscape is to be found, rather, in the "interspace." This is why landscape slips the grasp of ontology, of essence, of isolation, of the peculiar and the "assigned," and thus of the question "What is it?" (identification). It is through the generation of an *interspace* and, subsequently, of interaction and intensity that "land" becomes "landscape."

Also, properly speaking, the *variation* that sets landscape into tension reduces neither to "contrast" nor to "variety" our ordinary, ontology-dependent concepts. "Contrast" is too limited to the aspectual. It is too flat and resultative. It juxtaposes or "contraposes." "Variety" too falls short, though in Europe it is traditionally the first attribute bestowed on landscape (Fontenelle: "The charm of landscape lies in variety"[6]). The

---

5. François Jullien, *L'Écart et l'entre: Leçon inaugurale de la Chaire sur l'altérité* (Paris: Galilée, 2012).
6. *"La variété fait le charme du paysage."* [Translator's note.]

concept is limited to enumeration (in the West the old rhetorical notion of *varietas* is paired with oratorical "abundance," or *copia*) and thus reduces landscape to a mere collection of *objects* (Furetière as cited in the *Dictionnaire de Trévoux*: "Beautiful landscapes are diversified by a great quantity of objects pleasing to the eye, like hills, valleys, the countryside, prairies, woods, vines. . . . The more diverse the objects in a landscape, the more beautiful the landscape"[7]). *Variation*, by contrast, does not arise from additive thinking. It presumes a development. The notion is not tabular or spectacular but processual (in the manner of musical variation). Variety, we might say, "flattens things out" (into "objects") while variation "sets them into tension" (and gives rise to *polarities*). Whereas variety presumes identity (the identity of a "thing" or an essence, the basis of ontology) and proceeds therefrom to *unfold* the diverse like a fan, variation undermines all support for "Being," as a general category, and expresses only "effect" or what is "under way." This is why landscape is "interspace."

In the famous letter in *Julie, or the New Heloise* where he proceeds from "land" to "landscape" (promoting landscape from the land), Rousseau conceives of landscape only, I believe, through variation, although he actually speaks of "variety." Could this be because he had the cunning, or the sound intuition, to render his account of the landscape not with a tableau (a "view," a description, or a panorama) but with a development (an excursion and thus a narration)? In fact, the only notion Rousseau employs to structure the landscape is alternation: "Here immense rocks. . . . Here high and noisy waterfalls. . . . Here an eternal torrent." "Sometimes I would get lost in the dark of a thick wood. Sometimes, as I emerged from a chasm, a pleasant prairie would suddenly delight my eye."[8] Although "variety" is always on his lips, although he still speaks only and always of "blends," of "contrast," of "spectacle," and, at the beginning, of an "observer," with an old, declamatory, theatrical rhetoric (he calls nature a "real theater"), Rousseau does not overlook the landscape-ment produced by a tension-setting that he deems continuous and systematic (his sole rationale here). "Next to a cave were houses," and so forth. With Rousseau and the mountain we are actually beginning to discover what it means in Europe to "live off" landscape.

---

7. "*Les beaux paysages sont diversifiés par une grande quantité d'objets agréables à la vue, comme des collines, des vallées, des campagnes, des prairies, des bois, des vignes. . . . Plus il y a de divers objets dans un paysage, plus il est beau.*" [Translator's note.]

8. "*Tantôt d'immenses roches. . . . Tantôt de hautes et bruyantes cascades. . . . Tantôt un torrent éternel.*" "*Quelquefois, je me perdais dans l'obscurité d'un bois touffu. Quelquefois, en sortant d'un gouffre, une agréable prairie réjouissait tout à coup mes regards.*" [Translator's note.]

5

The great Tang Dynasty (eighth-century) poet Wang Wei, who was also a great painter, has bequeathed to us a marvelous page, a thoroughgoing treatise on the requirement of variation, titled "Secret Recipe for Mountains and Waters."[9] He begins it by saying that the art of landscape is to condense the world's tensions by concentrating opposites: "On a board one foot square draw a landscape of thousands of *li*: East—West—South—North are as if before your eyes; spring—summer—autumn—winter are born beneath the brush." (Recall Rousseau's aforementioned letter: "At dawn the flowers of spring, at noon the fruits of autumn, to the north the ice of winter: she [nature] was gathering all the seasons in the same instant, all climates in the same place."[10]) "As we begin by establishing the edges of the water," our Chinese painter continues, "we must not let the mountains drift." We begin, that is, not by framing the perspective but by ensuring that we anchor the primary tension and variation, between mountain and water. "Then, as you fork the paths, let no path unfold continuously." Indeed, roads must disappear and reappear farther on; their interruption, in varying and breaking the monotony, puts tension into the relief through a stepping back.

Unlike Albertian composition, which arranges and assembles parts along a progressive scale, from small to large (for the human body it proceeds from the "surface" to the member, the body, and the "story"), Wang Wei's painting develops end to end through a correlation of opposites, which, like an undulation, discreetly engender *tension by variation*:

> The welcoming summit should rise to eminence;
> the welcomed summits should crowd around it.

As for dwellings:

> In the folds of the mountains one can erect hermitages;
> at the water's edge one can set the dwellings of people.

The one responds to the other, is warranted only because it introduces variation and tension with its other, in a vis-à-vis. Where the landscape opens, at "water's edge," you set activity; where it closes, in the "fold," you set life that has withdrawn. The entire painting develops along these lines, in successive polarities. Nothing "is," but everything *correlates*.

---

9. "*Shanshuilun*," in *Zhongguo hualun leibian* (abbr. *Leibian*), ed. Yu Jianhua (Beijing: Zhonggua shuju, 1973), 596.

10. "*Au levant les fleurs du printemps, au midi les fruits de l'automne, au nord les glaces de l'hiver : elle [la nature] réunissait toutes les saisons dans le même instant, tous les climats dans le même lieu.*" [Translator's note.]

Every new pairing, held aloft by the coupling of utterances, sets a new tension that crisscrosses the others:

> Around the village, cluster trees to form a wood:
> the branches must envelop the trunk.
> In the hollow of the ravine, focus a cascading stream:
> do not allow the torrent to fall haphazardly.

There is thus no other way to "assemble" a landscape, no other way for variation to weave its tentacular way in through the pairings and allow for respiratory circulation. We must have both the single and the multiple (trees/stream), just as we must have both the inhabited and the wild (the village/the ravine). This same exigency must be continuously prolonged, from one notation to the next. At the same time, each pole must be sufficiently *consistent*, by internal coherence (I return to these terms)—the tree trunk densely swathed in branches and the stream resisting any dispersion)—for tension to arise between them.

There are thus two dimensions of variation in which landscape weaves together and enters into tension. On the one hand, we have breadth, and the potency of its divide, as between mountain and water. On the other, we have multiplicity, the crisscrossing and intersection of many divides, and their resulting *density*. Both intensity and diversity are characteristic of variation. A single big opposition (confrontation of elements)—between sea and sky, for instance—is not enough. Out in the open sea, where one sees nothing but sea and sky, there is a sublime view of extreme simplicity, but I have already wondered whether it would qualify as landscape (even if I were a seaman). Landscape is promoted when variation tautens into a network and forms a net. In China the mountain is in this sense exemplary. It is the abode of all contraries: not only between the face in shadow and the face in the light (yin and yang, and ubac and adret) but also between the massive base and the slender apex, or between the wooded and the bare, the rocky and the grassy, the exposed and the withdrawn, the deserted and the inhabited, and what is chiseled and jutting and what is veiled in clouds. The mountain acquires consistency also only insofar as the brush indefinitely varies it, the inky wash alternating the "empty" with the "full," the "dense" with the "sparse," the "pale" with the "concentrated," the "light" with the "heavy," and so forth.

This sort of variation *vitalizes*. It incites, activates, and deploys exchange. And it does so in and of itself, by setting up polarities whose alternation calls forth renewal. (Recall that China has devoted more thought to respiration than to perception.) If the singularization from which landscape proceeds gives rise to ("un-mires") a sense of *existence*, the variation that sets landscape into tension takes the sense of "being alive" ("living"/"existing": the former extending into metaphysics, the latter plunging into the organic) and lifts it to a higher plane. I would therefore say that landscape, even as it gains breadth through variation, intensifies the sense of being alive by restoring interior tension. This is also—or primarily—why we "live off landscape." And I wonder whether this is not what Rousseau hints at in the famous passage above ("one breathes more easily"[11]). Couldn't he be referring to the more "pure and rarified" air of mountain summits? It seems to me easy to believe that all of the contrasts he trots out take part in this activation of vitality—discreetly, to be sure, but so effectively that we do not see it, and no longer detect the awareness of the physiological.

In China the life-intensifying variation of landscape carries over even into the art of dwelling. I particularly like the way the Tang scholar Liu Zongyuan, a contemporary of Wang Wei's, designed his *house for living*. He set it in a landscape that encourages him to "forget" the world, because it varies the house with the time of day.[12] "I've selected the dwelling's north room and opened up the right side to make it an evening room; I've selected the east room of the stage[13] and opened up the left side to make it a morning room; and I've subsequently opened it up on the north side to make it a shade room and arranged a room under the north window to make a solarium; I've built the pavilion in the center to make a central room." By reversing every room's use—morning room in the evening, evening room in the morning, and center room still at noon—our scholar could double the possibilities. For "in the shade room I take shelter from hot wind; in the solarium I take shelter from icy wind." "If there is neither great cold nor a heat wave, however, then morning and evening return to their nominal use." The house itself, though a symbol of stability and fixity (a "dwelling" we call it), takes us on a journey through landscape, by diversification of its sites. Rather than have its "composition" syntactically marshaled by a hierarchy of functional differences (primary room and secondary rooms, each with its own purpose), a house is designed in a completely paratactic, juxtapositional, and substitutive way: like an unfolded system of opposed but equivalent units, multiplicative of *variation*.

6

One variation in particular, noted by all Chinese treatises on painting, is essential to landscape: that of the "near" and the "far" (近远). We need all

---

11. "*On se sent plus de facilité dans la respiration.*" [Translator's note.]
12. Liu Zongyuan, "*Liu zhuo dong ting ji,*" in *Liu Hedong ji*, 472.
13. Stage in the sense of a way station. [Translator's note.]

three of the following to make a landscape: *singularization*, which brings out an individual kernel to promote "existing"; *variation*, which activates vitality, not only by what it sets into tension but also by the exchange and transformation it engenders; and *remove*, which opens an escape and encourages a going-beyond. Remove produces a flaring out. It prolongs, calls on us to carry on farther still. It de-specifies, clears out and opens up [*dégage*], decants, and opens onto indeterminacy and infinitude. It opens, between being and nonbeing, a space for "vagueness," and thereby encourages "pensiveness" and "reflection." It unmoors thought. This is the very vocation of landscape that fosters "living": it deploys and disengages. For living is not just a matter of alternation-exchange, in the manner of metabolism. Living, however it might be expressed, is also a matter of passing into the other, of leaving and separating from the "self," and of reaching for the beyond and pushing the envelope. It is at once to unfence and to become. Landscape's remove *conveys*—our languages express it so poorly—this vagueness and aspiration.

And thus I return to a previous point: that landscape is defined primarily in opposition to the garden. A garden can lack remove (the "curate's garden"). As its Indo-European etymology (*ghorto*, from the Latin *hortus*) suggests—although it is found in other cultures as well—the garden is preferably an enclosed place. It is set apart from the surrounding land. It is cut off and establishes an interior. It depends on having a limit, thanks to which nature can take shelter, perfect itself, and refine itself. What distinguishes the garden from landscape is therefore not so much size as the presence of a *border* (*hortus conclusus* by definition). A garden is contained and walled in, whereas a landscape is by vocation what will not be enclosed or contained. There is no landscape except through opening, spacing out, and transitioning toward the beyond.

I wonder, therefore, whether in choosing the "horizon" for our basis, as we have ordinarily done in Europe, we are not already restricting the scope of our definition of landscape—at least if we think of a literal horizon, the limit of the expanse that from a certain position lies within a subject's view ("the circular line of sight for an observer who stands at its center"). The "horizon" as "limit" or definition (*horismos*, ὁρισμός, in Greek) is already a sort of enclosure. However, by thinking precisely in these terms—if we conceive of landscape on the basis of such a circumscription, beyond which nothing is visible, and immediately separate with this demarcation the visible and the invisible into two distinct spaces—we are already overlooking landscape's *continuous remove*, already under way and deepening in successive planes. Little by little, as it gradually unfolds, this remove erases contours while at the same time dissipating presence by increasing "vagueness."

The choice of demarcation—at least insofar as it underlies the "horizon"—is not without consequence. It is by no means obvious how the notion of delimitation carries over into landscape. Indeed, it is perhaps one of the reasons that the Greeks overlooked landscape-thought. From the beginning both their knowledge and their ethics led them to trace the "limit," *peras*, which saved them from indeterminacy and thus from the inconsistency of the unlimited, *apeiron* (ἄπειρον), or of hubris (ὕβρις). Nondemarcation was to them frightful. They could achieve knowledge and control only by marking the beginning and end of things (*arché-télos*); only in this way could they legitimate the *logos*. They would apprehend by "defining." They thought they could immediately draw the line of separation between the knowable and the unknowable, being and nonbeing, or the visible and the invisible. For the Greeks—because they sought in geometry to construct space through intersecting planes, and in metaphysics to ascribe to the invisible a status of intelligibility that separated it a priori from the sensible—the visible would easily be led into its corral. Corralling it, in fact, was the only way to maintain its integrity. They also conceived of an "over there," *ekei*, separate from the visible, the Over-There of Elsewhere. They took advantage of its status of absence, and Platonism eagerly projects it into another world (of health or truth). But the Greeks did not conceive of progressive remove as a continual process extending out from proximity and trailing off little by little into the indistinct.

7

Instead of allowing ourselves to get caught up right away at its edge, at its limit, why not experience landscape as we would experience anything else: in its gradual unfolding (in its processual deployment)? Landscape will no longer abide circumscription by a horizon line, or an immediate cutoff at its extremity. It will now offer itself up as a deepening, as an endless penetration, inviting the eye to lose its way within. But to do this must we trade the Greek landscape, where summits and coasts stand out from an azure ground, for a landscape of monsoons, where mountains are forever bathed in humidity, swathed in a nimbus of vapors that scale the valleys and "melt" form (融, as Chinese notably puts it)? I sometimes come across the term *horizon* in European translations of ancient Chinese treatises, but whenever I then check the original text the Chinese word is nowhere to be found. This is intriguing. Might this "lack" in Chinese be concealing something (something we do not know how to think)? Or, rather, might it subtly be hinting at a divide—an anecdotal divide, one might say at first—whose cleft we ought to plumb?

For instance, it is common in Chinese to say, "Ascend high and go to the extreme of the view" (登高極目). The activity here concerns the eye, not a contemplated territory whose ultimate extension is marked by a "horizon." It is the eye that is pushed to the limit of its possibilities. Hence the following elaboration on the "distant mountains": "You arrange things in such a way that those who contemplate them, projecting their gaze as far as it will go, struggle to exhaust."[14] "There thus arise in them" "thoughts from the corners of the sea and the shores of the sky" (海角天涯); and "it is then that one begins to savor the distant mountains." This is far from having the horizon serve as the limit of a landscape thus determined (the expanse perceived from the position of a subject). Instead, it designates the ends or the confines of the world, and through them takes the landscape contemplated in a painting and opens it up to its extreme—or, better yet, brings it to a going-beyond. In this way a landscape "does not grow wearisome" (will not be "exhausted by the eye"). By "savoring" it in this way we enter into *contemplation*, begin to "dream" about it.

What we have here is a cultural experience that, in contradicting our notion of a "horizon," leads us to consider the remote as a *prolongation without end*. The painter Guo Xi was already pointing the way when he invoked the "far-off ground"[15] or said that "the peaks and summits multiply and accumulate." Through this linking-together "the landscape up and dissipates," "we do not tire of the remove," and "the eye is opened to the extreme of immensity." Remoteness as an unfolding of successive planes that push on into infinity, where the eye can lose its way, and that bring us closer not to the delimitation of things—the method of *knowledge*—but to their original confusion is what makes landscape the natural point of departure, and the medium, for meditation. (By contrast, we might say that the meditation in question is about *existence*.) A poem by the first great landscape poet, Xie Lingyun,[16] begins like this:

[On] foot	go out	[to] the west	wall	gate,
[In the] distance	contemplate	[from the] wall	[to] the west	summits:
linked	successive planes	stacked	repeated	in layers,
green	blue	confused	deep	immerse [oneself].

---

14. Zhang Dai, *Hui shi fa wei*, in *Hualun Congkan*, 1:248.
15. That is, *ground* as it functions in the terms *foreground* and *background*, though *fore-* and *back-* are doubtless too limited, too binary, for what Jullien has in mind. [Translator's note.]
16. Xie Lingyun, *"Wan chu xi shi tang shi."*

Accepting the Chinese word's invitation, we must follow along as the *inward push* proceeds, trailing off in its endlessness. What is evoked is not a horizon distinguishable to the eye but only an unlimited piling/flaring-out of layers of mountains, somber and murky (*yao*, 杳), melting away into infinity, and in which both our vision and our thought allow themselves to be absorbed. This dilution of any demarcation or horizon line plunges us into an indistinct end of things. It triggers a reconsideration of the "self," but one that in the rest of the poem spills over from the "self" and turns back on its experience. By comparison with the plunge into the world's endlessness, this reconsideration can concern only the self's fragility, its lonesomeness, aging, and withering. Against this push into the fundamental confusion of things, as even the poet concludes, any words of grand moral pretention would be vain. Better to be "apart," to "devote oneself to the zither's song." Better to allow oneself to be carried along, in one's intimacy, by variation alone. Or, as another great poet, Xi Kang, put it not long before, in two verses famous for the contrast they set up between the far and the near ("sight"/"hand," always a polarity), "The hand brushing the five strings / The eye follows the wild geese as they take flight."

8

In his "Secret Recipe for Mountains and Waters," painter Wang Wei presents the same notion of painted remove:

> The distant summits with vapors rising from the valleys unite;
> the distant sky and the water's dazzle trade their gleam.[17]

Rather than have a demarcation (here again the translation misleadingly adds an expected "horizon"), the vague remove makes way for communication and fusion: "The far-off scene is being shrouded in fog, and the clouds are enclosing the deep cliffs." Moreover, the remove is painted not by delimitation but by *effacement*. To cite a much-borrowed passage from Wang Wei,

> The distant men are without eyes,
> the distant trees are without branches,
> the distant mountains are without rocks:
> appearing hardly as eyelashes;
> the distant waters are without waves:
> at the same height as the clouds.[18]

---

17. Wang Wei, "*Shanshuijue,*" in *Leibian,* 592.
18. Wang Wei, "*Shanshuilun,*" in *Leibian,* 596.

Remove, then, leads not to the frontier of the invisible (what a "horizon" would mark) but to the *scarcely perceptible*, in the manner of delicate eyebrows. It leads, that is, to the edge of blurring.

The same goes for what Michel Collot has called the "internal horizon": parts that are hidden from view, not at the horizon but within the field of vision. Wang Wei is always harking back to this but in order to drain the reality from the depiction, mark it with absence, space it out, and open it to its going-beyond:

> The mountainsides are clogged with clouds,
> the rocky cliffs are clogged with waterfalls,
> towers and terraces are clogged with trees,
> roads and paths are clogged with people.[19]

Covered ("clogged" to the eye, hidden, 塞) hints and leaves us guessing. Rather than impose it, the covering decants presence, makes it allusive, and deploys its spiritual and aural dimension. A whole—uncovered—presence is therefore opaque. It immobilizes in a "being there" that is henceforth only "that." Thus it is said that one must paint "as if there were and as if there were not"—at the transition of the two, confounding ontology—and such as to make presence emerge through its withdrawal:

> Of millstones and earthen levees only a half shall be shown;
> of thatched cottages and reed pavilions present only a patch of wall or of cornice.[20]

Blurring the distant and burying the proximate amount to the same thing in painting. The idea is not to set the visible and the invisible in opposition but to unburden the visible of, or free it from, whatever lies within that tends to enclose or reify it. The idea is to extract it from whatever would confine it in its own "being," enclose it in the weight of its "thingness," or reduce it to "inertia," such as to bring out once more the inner élan that pervades it and puts it in touch with its core of invisibility or infinity.

Because there is no break between the visible and the invisible, and because there is thus no planar rupture between two levels of Being (where one would become the other's image and reproduction), this going-beyond of the visible is not symbolic. It occurs not through a doubling (visible/intelligible: hence the possibility of a symbol) but—to use a term I have adopted for lack of a better one—*by overflow*. What produces this gradual overflow is not just the distant blurring of the limit but the

---

19. Ibid.
20. Wang Wei, "Shanshuijue," 592.

(it seems to me) more audacious opening of a remoteness *within proximity itself*. Internal spacing-out, opening up from a landscape's interior, detaches the landscape from its realism without abandoning its sensible quality. I find it remarkable that it is through and on the subject of painting that these thinkers should have developed one of Chinese thought's most interesting contributions: internal transcendence by flaring, freed from the limits of the sensible yet not abandoning the sensible altogether.

It is said that Wang Wei painted "banana trees amid snow."[21] This sort of dissonance within the sensible produces the effect of a dehiscence and subsequently suffices to provoke a dis-adherence with the condition of things (with their character in terms of properties and exclusion) but without tipping depiction into the representation of some other thing, in the manner of ideas, to be conceived figuratively and symbolically on an abstract plane. Moreover, as a seventeenth-century commentator on poetry (Wang Shizhen) points out, the same principle applies to the poems of Wang Wei in which places too far apart to be apprehended simultaneously by the eye are joined in one landscape. This spatial impossibility, our critic concludes, leads us to approach such a landscape "otherwise than by strict topography"[22] (by the tool that measures kilometers, to be exact). In other words, *assemblage*, which we now recognize as the elemental fact of landscape (as what makes land into landscape), is neither reducible to the visual (empirical) nor ideal (constructed or abstract) but proceeds from what Chinese calls an "incitement," provoking an "encounter" by a "subtle going-beyond" (i.e., beyond strict phenomenality; this is my attempt to render as faithfully as possible the phrase *xing hui chao miao*, 兴会超妙). Landscape, in the intensity of the encounter that it constitutes (that constitutes it), un-mires itself from (escapes its enclosure in) the gloomy, supposedly objective exiguity of space. Under the effect of the remoteness opening up within its very interior, landscape distends and breaks free of the horizon's confines. In this way it can pluck the visible from slackness and restore it to *soaring*. And at the same time, we confirm that landscape is no longer a "corner" of the world.

A Chinese commentator on poetry elevates into a motto the following passage from the *Zhuangzi*: "Those who accompany him turn back at the cliff; he at the same cliff distances himself."[23] "Distance oneself"—take a step back to get some perspective. "Where to" goes unsaid, and perhaps there is no "where to." But why value a remoteness *that begins*, or else what kind of possibility *opens up* from the mere act of *setting off*? The passage speaks of "abandoning the ordinary world," of the start of a

---

21. Wang Shizhen, "Zhu xing lei," in *Daijingtang shihua*, Renmin wenxue chubanshe, Beijing, 1963, p. 67 s.
22. Ibid., §3.
23. Wang Shizhen, "Ru shen lei," in *Daijingtang shihua*, §1, 69.

solitary trek that, in prompting a clearing-out and opening-up [*dégagement*] within the world and removing the world's limit, renders the world inexhaustible and thus, as the Chinese language puts it, "indefinitely savorable"—just as "words have an end but meaning does not." This way of allowing remoteness to emerge within proximity and un-miring the world with the aura of beyond-ness, but without building up the beyond into a dualist credo or making it into the object of a conversion, contains a finely wrought coherence that clearly aims to deploy living—or, as we have already said, the "art of living." But we must reawaken the dormant expression. It develops from the *Zhuangzi*'s thought to reflections on painting and poetry. It is, in fact, a deft strategy, one carved right out of landscape and intended to draw the world out of its inertia, to draw life out of its atony.

9

Liu Xie noted (in his sixth-century commentary on landscape's advent in poetry[24]) that "when the teachings of the *Zhuangzi* were removed"—that is, when "Taoism," as in the third century, after the Han Dynasty's fall, ceased to be zealously taught and discussed, because the crumbling bureaucracy from which it offered the sole escape (worldly withdrawal) was no more—"landscape began to flourish." In other words, the development of landscape-thought as a flaring of the visible, as the deployment of remoteness within the sensible itself, took the torch from Taoist teaching. It transferred Taoism's aspirations for going-beyond to what we now call nature. In China, then, the advent of landscape corresponds to a particular *moment* (in the fourth to fifth century), just as it does in Europe (the sixteenth century), although for entirely different reasons. And our landscape-thought has been torn ever since, has it not? I cannot elude the question much longer: can we take Chinese landscape-thought, predating as it does the ontology of (European) science, and repatriate it today into *our* thought? This is another way of asking whether it has not by now become isolated, grown over, and obsolete.

The question, then, is whether landscape-thought belongs to singular cultural moments that stand apart from one another, and trap it in bubbles. Does it belong to the fourth- and fifth-century Chinese scholar explaining in terms of the great welcoming tension of "mountains and waters" that the time of a now-unlivable political order has passed? Or does it belong to the European subject of the Renaissance whose eye dominates

---

24. From the commentary of Wang Shizhen, "*Qing yan lei*," Remin wenxue chubanshe, Beijing, 1963, p. 87 s.

a now-homogeneous expanse and sets the horizon with respect to his position? Could we, despite a dispersion that is equal parts ideological and historical, produce a *concept of landscape*? Or do the "reasons of landscape" (Augustin Berque) close in on themselves severally, like successive waves separated by a Before and an After (the modernity ushered in by Western physics)? Has Chinese reason been displaced by new knowledge?

In China, landscape serves to posit an opening to the world that does not rid itself of the sensible but renders it more alert (less inert) and evasive-intensive. In Europe, meanwhile, it "serves" as a territory of conquest and expansion for the vision of an individual who objectively "observes" and "represents" it, thanks to optics and geometry, and then invests it with pathos (nostalgia) to compensate for his lost subjectivity. But suppose we were prepared to erect a concept of landscape that confronted such diverse cultural perspectives to each other at their crossroads, reflected them off each other (this is not "comparison"), and could thus transform landscape into an experience henceforth to be lived by *all* of humanity (such, as we all know, is the criterion of universal philosophy). This would lead us to observe that Chinese reflections on landscape had elucidated aspects of what "gives rise to landscape" to which we in Europe had given less consideration, our theoretical choices having led us elsewhere. Once we had developed their coherence, moreover, philosophical reason would *open up* and be ready to benefit from these aspects. At least, I claim, if it managed to "open up": that is, if it underwent a deconstruction of its language and categories sufficient to render those aspects accessible. Otherwise it would likely dismiss this Chinese insight as outmoded, because of being crushed beneath the triumphant physics of Europe's Âge Classique,[25] or else relegate it to a fascinating exoticism—the sort of thing we so readily indulge in nowadays when seeking to compensate for science's "hard" objectivity or enjoy some anodyne amusement.

10

We have grounds to believe (or at least a hint of evidence, as I see it) that a transcultural, transhistorical, philosophically useful concept of landscape is possible, and that we needn't settle for the idea that landscape, like a moment in art, is the product of a culturally and historically limited artialization. It would not be very difficult to find in Europe's own *evocation* of landscape a conception of landscape as *tension-setting*, itself arising from

---

25. This period corresponds roughly to the late seventeenth and early eighteenth centuries in France: that is, just before the Enlightenment. [Translator's note.]

such conjoint effects as I have just mentioned. I mean by this the way in which European writers have themselves approached landscape, even if the coherencies do not emerge so cleanly in their theoretical reflections, or indeed if the coherencies are thwarted, because contravened by other biases (the "gaze," the "subject," the "horizon," etc.). And so I find myself *in fine* undertaking to reread European "landscape," approaching it from outside its definition, going outside its frame, or, I dare say, examining it "in the Chinese manner." I will be revealing what can be "lived" within it yet remain imprecise, and even what can constitute a system within it yet only in passing, without fanfare. The rereading, that is, that I have begun in Rousseau.

It proceeds, venturing further out, in Stendhal (from Rousseau to Stendhal: is this the extent of my thinking?). I find the first page of *The Red and the Black* lacking. It is too descriptive, too given to the picturesque. I find it a somewhat wheezing, because obligatory, way to start the novel (which is nonetheless the most beautiful of novels). The evocation of Lake Como in *The Charterhouse of Parma*, meanwhile, is a whole other matter. (In this respect the page is in fact decisive.) *Evocation* is apt here because driven by an *encounter*—or rather by a reunion (the countess returns to the setting of her childhood). The tension set up in the sensible is general and leads to a convergence of all previously envisaged effects. Indeed, it is no exaggeration to say that Stendhal transformed Lake Como into *his* landscape. Remove "eye," "satisfied," or "astonished," and descriptive rhetoric remains. Here we can clearly conceive of living off landscape, with no hint of any lack. Or, rather, any suggested absence forms a natural part of the satisfaction. The landscape is, moreover, (re)discovered by two people. The page is worth a fresh look: "The countess, with Fabrice, looked out once more over all the enchanting lands surrounding Grianta, and so celebrated by travelers."

The *tension-setting* lies first in the configuration of settings: between the imposing chateau and Villa Melzi in vis-à-vis, and especially between the two branches of the lake, the "so voluptuous" Como branch and the branch "that runs toward Lecco, all severity." "Sublime and graceful" aspects, concludes Stendhal, ratcheting the tension up so high as to verge on contradiction. There is *singularization* at work particularly in the chiseling of the relief: in "those hills of unequal height" and "those hills of wondrous shape, plunging down to the lake with such singular slopes" (the intensive "such" is key). This *stepping back*, moreover, conjures presence, which is brought into play by the covered (the "obstructed"): "The villages halfway along the shore are hidden by great trees"; they show "above the summits of the trees" with their "lovely belfries." Variation deepens through discontinuity: "If from time to time some small field, fifty paces wide, interrupts the clumps of chestnut and wild-cherry trees.

. . ." *Remove*, in a word, provides matter for pensiveness. This is not just the remove that one perceives by pitching one's gaze farther off, into the beyond of snow-capped peaks, and "recalling" with a turn back into the self "the measure of life's misfortunes that one requires to increase the present moment's sensual delight," but also, and more importantly, the *heard* remove, "the distant sound of a bell in some small village." This prompts us to reflect on what amounts not only to a true commonplace but also to the only truth that remains once we have parsed all the others: the truth that life "slips away" and that it behooves us not to put off any longer our long-awaited enjoyment. We *sojourn* in the proffered retreat ("hermitages where we would all like to dwell") even more than we "contemplate," to use the famous verb. Stendhal adds a final stroke to the others on his page, but it is less another stroke than the motivation for all the others. I will call it *connivance* and conclude by explaining it.

VIII

Connivance

1

We drag behind us a theme as old as our nascent modernity, the theme of "communion with nature," and we are encumbered with its pathos (its romantic exclamation). It encumbers us intellectually because we cannot help but see in it a sign of what European reason has repressed: namely, the wedge that it boldly and triumphantly drove between what would become nature's "objectivity" (i.e., what would come to constitute "nature")—which, through science, gave us purchase on nature—and what dug itself in on the far side of the cleft as the subjectivity of consciousness and feeling (Cartesian "thought"). European reason triumphed, that is, when it promoted a physics that was mathematical in language, separating itself from the phenomenality of things (to which the old physics adhered) and severing all ties of complicity with the vital. Thus the term *communion* came to serve as a sort of reparation. But it is evident how easily, and irreparably, it could lead to what must thenceforth be irrationalism: defiance (denial) of reason and its authority, or at best an escape from what science had overly clarified. "Literature," by gathering up what science dropped or rendered unrecognizable in our experience, gave voice to this—thus our encumbering "communion with nature." We cannot be rid of it, because it is the only plaster covering the fissure.

But there is another relation to the world, one that I will call *connivance*. Connivance stakes a rightful claim opposite knowledge. It recovers what knowledge has ended up repressing, though not quite abolishing, and from this opposite position demonstrates the coherence of what has been repressed. (It is also a way to stand apart from Paul Claudel's insufficient *"co-naissance,"*[1] with its vindictive mysticism.) Knowledge has evolved into speculative knowledge (i.e., knowledge for its own sake) and in so doing has, via science, foresworn any need to adapt to the world of its birth. In becoming it own end knowledge has disengaged from the vital. It therefore now confers on us the strictly correlative task of reconsidering the relation that reason has covered up but that still maintains our tacit understanding with things, though it now operate in the shadows. This "understanding," however, escapes our awareness. It remains implicit, lying beneath the relational work undertaken by reason. We will prove unable to elucidate it unless we compel reason to retrace its steps, go back into its history, in order to explore what it has separated itself from: not things it has heroically fought against (obscurantism opposing the Enlightenment) but things that, in the righteous and mighty battle to impose itself, reason could only allow to escape—what now lies dormant in our *un-known*, and thus escapes our intelligence. If *knowledge*, as we know, stands in opposition to ignorance, what stands in contradiction to knowledge is *connivance*. They stand on equal footing but also back to back. The Latin *connivere* means to come to an understanding "with a wink."

In isolating something called "nature" and setting it up as an "object," science seems to use methodical abstraction to make one space the same as any other (as in the Cartesian expanse), just as it projects a uniform and charted sort of time. If so, then we also know, in a way that needs no proof, what "escapes" science. We know that *living*, by contrast, supposes a mode of intelligence or apprehension—or, more radically, "caption"[2]— that weaves its web day by day, without our thinking about it and without our thinking to think about it, and maintains *adherence*—rather than introducing distance or urging us to make distinctions. Indeed, we end up suspecting that knowledge developed through science is but the visible side of a coin that exists only because of the ever-present but separate *conniving flipside*. It is a shadowy knowledge that remains integrated in a milieu, that will not be drawn out of its condition, that separates no "me" from the "world," and that remains beneath all exposition—all explanation. It will not be abstracted from a "landscape."

A child at its mother's bosom or on her lap has practically no other knowledge than that. (Or in the usual comparison, early cultures are more *conniving*; later cultures, more *knowledgeable*.) Then, with school, as

---

1. Definition from the Centre National de Resources Textuelles et Lexicales: "co-naissance (from the verb *co-naître*), fem. noun, literary. [In Claudel] 'To know oneself [*se connaître*] is to make oneself the means of co-birth [*co-naissance*]; for a living being this means to give birth to, as with the being's own self, all the objects known to said being and of which said being is the common image' ([Paul] Claudel, *Art poétique*, 1907, p. 182)." [Translator's note.]

2. In the old sense of seizure, or the modern sense (in electronics) of reception. The French term here is *captage*. [Translator's note.]

the written word flattens and equalizes, and knowledge is divided into disciplines, "objects" take shape and come into isolation; planes are separated that reason must once more bind together. The conniving relation is covered up as soon as a knowledgeable subject wins its autonomy, but it does not vanish. It persists in silence, buried, tacit, like a water table ready to surface. Landscape is that surfacing. In truth, I live my life by passing discreetly from one to the other, partaking of this agility. I progress (assert myself) in *knowledge* or step back, regress from my autarchic self, in *connivance*. Or let us say that I am more knowledgeable when I go out (in public) and more conniving when I "go home" (intimate speech). Or else I am made knowledgeable by science and returned to a state of connivance by poetry (at least when said poetry is operative). Yet this conniving relation, kept as it is in the shadows, contained and held back, would have no place of its own to promote it within the world if "landscape" did not appear. Whereas with "land" I am knowledgeable, with a landscape I *return to a state of connivance.*

2

Thus there is "landscape"—this is my new, and final, definition—when my capacity for knowledge shifts (inverts) into *connivance* and when my objectivating relation with the world changes into understanding and tacit communication. Properly speaking, I do not "personify" the landscape's elements or "project" myself into them, nor do I lend my subjectivity to things or animate the inanimate. The subject still holds itself to be master in all such operations, and thus they remain facile. What occurs instead is a genuine transmutation. When land becomes landscape I am no longer indifferent to what I apprehend. What I see in the landscape beckons to me, "speaks to me," and "touches me," in the familiar phrase (can we avoid such familiarity?). We are feeling our way forward as we advance these expressions; they demand clarification. In other words, what I apprehend promotes itself into partnership, and the tension-setting that singularizes what I apprehend welcomes me in and urges me to partake. There is landscape when land allows itself to be *encountered*. There is landscape, that is, when a relationship is established (reestablished) with the world such that I can push on upstream from the relationship established by knowledgeable reason, when I can seek out the source underneath; there is landscape when the *place* suddenly becomes a "link."

The experience of landscape interests me philosophically because it pries apart our traditional, codified opposition between reason and its official counterpart: that is, between "reason" and "passion," or even "reason" and "emotion." It is a garrulous opposition, and one that clings to the surface. It reveals underneath my deeper rootedness in the world. It obliterates my ordinary relation to said world (the relation that exists when there is only "land"), a relation of which I would otherwise have no conception. Truth be told, I would otherwise never even suspect it. By suspending in and through landscape my function as a knowing-acting subject ("understanding"—"will": the great pairing of traditional reason)—by suspending the function by which I am intellectually and socially constituted—I unearth this more elementary connection. In landscape we happen upon this connection, and like a wellspring it gushes suddenly forth (fulfilling an aspiration that we no longer knew we had). At the same time, there is no fusional shift, no compensatory slide into the ecstatic or the mystic. I succumb to no irrationalism (we are dealing with what lies upstream from reason, not polemically denying reason). With regard to irrationalism our famous "communion" with nature was, we must admit, rather dubious.

Through landscape and the connivance on my part that I discover in it I am reacquainted with the world at a more primordial level. By embracing the singular individuation that sets the world in tension and promotes it into landscape I find myself coming closer to the root of my own individuation. I find myself more securely anchored, *grafted*, in my relation to the world. Landscape's peculiarity is to make me belong to the world. I no longer relate to the world at a particular place (finding myself on mere "land") but reconnect with the world in itself (with its totality). In landscape I reconnect with *what gives rise to world-ness*. What gives rise to "landscape" is my going from a local dependence (the place where I am; I am always somewhere) to *global belonging*, such that my passage into the latter becomes sensible. There is landscape when we no longer see only perceived objects—objects composing it in a more or less disparate manner—and instead are introduced, as in a revelation, to that through which the world is world. Landscape arises when a given piece of land, singular as it is, "assembles" itself, as it does, and *becomes world*. In this way it no longer falls short. It no longer runs up against its limit, the limit that would set it off as a "part" or that the "horizon" lays down. At that point we can delight indefinitely in a landscape.

3

The landscape, in Stendhal's great comparison, is a *bow* "that played upon my soul." In other words, no self-subject projects itself into the landscape, turning it into an emotional confidant (the banal posture of bad romanticism). Rather, landscape singularizes itself and thereby draws me into its tensional field, in resonance with its variation. Here the phrase "my soul" introduces no conventional or compensatory lyricism. It refers simply to the more elementary capacity that emerges from beneath the declaredly autonomous spirit (the insular subject of knowledge and will) and makes itself known in a reactive and vital way (through "vibration") when it encounters a world that is *returning to a state of connivance*. This is a singular "encounter" but an encounter with something that needn't be exceptional (Proust's three threes). The landscape in question needn't be as rich in splendorous tensions as our Italian lake. On his plodding return to the Jura it is enough for him to glimpse "the line of cliffs on the way to Arbois, I think, and on the main road back from Dôle" (*The Life of Henry Brulard*). It is enough for singularity to arise from what had previously been mere "land," plucking it from indifference and providing with its aura the stuff of dreams ("Reverie is what I have sought above all else"), in like manner as the "soul" of the beloved woman ("Métilde"), who comes to stand out from all those around her.

Because of the connivance that resurfaces in my relation to the world, the landscape becomes "my" landscape; the place becomes a "link." Or rather, what this connivance reveals is that I have from time immemorial been linked to the landscape that I have happened upon. I cannot help but attribute to a shared past the sudden intimacy of my reaction, as if I were already nostalgic for the landscape (and past the point of renunciation). Such was Nietzsche's *encounter* with the Engadin: "True, there are many grander and finer pieces of scenery, but this [*diess*: always in the singular] is so familiar and intimate [*innig und vertraut*] to me, related by blood, nay even more to me!" ("The Wanderer and His Shadow," §338).[3] We expect to encounter such a landscape, and the expectation, though below our awareness, is such that it feels atavistic when the day finally arrives: "Now I have taken possession of the Engadin, and feel I am in my element" (letter to Overbeck). "My element" bespeaks the elemental relation to "living," a relation outside of which I can indeed hardly imagine that I could survive. Note, moreover, that Nietzsche does not say "landscape," *Landschaft*, whose usual meaning doubtless struck him as too narrowly visual, but *Natur-gegend*, "my natural surroundings," which, for him as for any other living being, becomes his *milieu*.

Yet I wonder whether in positing landscape as a "region" in which to live, *Gegend*, where an errant, sickly man such as he could at last regain some vitality, Nietzsche is not, at least at the start, still bound by a tether he cannot cut to a classical notion of the self and the world, a notion that landscape-thought ought to have destroyed. He begins by saying, "In some country places we rediscover ourselves, with a delightful shudder:

---

3. From *Human, All Too Human*, part 2, translated by Paul V. Cohn (1911). [Translator's note.]

it is the pleasantest way of finding our 'double.'"[4] But in a landscape—that is, in what "gives rise to landscape"—does nature actually reveal itself to be our "double" (*Doppelgängerei der Natur*, as he called it)? Does landscape arise when I recognize myself in it, such that it becomes another "me" and I see myself reflected back? Do I contemplate myself in a landscape as a narcissist? If so, then landscape does not take me out of myself. It does not cut into my autarchic self-subject (my *knowing* subject). There is thus no "encounter," and the affinity that supposedly results is in fact nothing but artifice.

If we dare not abandon the notion of a subject that is solid through and through and retains its autonomy, and if we then approach landscape from the subject's auto-consistency, henceforth no better than a "mirror" or "double," I believe we will once again fail to understand, from the phenomenological perspective, landscape's initializing function within the Subject. That function is precisely to provide the subject with a (precious) incitement to seek out its own headwaters, to head upstream from its position as "subject." It is to emancipate the subject, at least temporarily, from that position. It is to keep the subject from projecting itself into the landscape, as from determining the cut of the "horizon" from its position. What landscape does with respect to living is reopen a breach in the self-possession (self-sufficiency) of a "self." It accomplishes this by raising the "self" to a more primordial stage of its involvement in the world, where a properly *knowing* "subject," seeing itself as such, has yet to take shape; this is a stage where a subject has not yet dug itself in and withdrawn *into opposition to the world*. *Connivance* is the expression of this stage.

4

This is a question I still ask with respect to contemporary analyses (I owe the most illuminating exposition to Michel Collot[5]). These have sought to avoid both conceiving landscape through pure objectivation, like classical reason, and attributing it to the Subject, as Romanticism ended up doing. Instead they have sought to situate landscape between the two, considered that landscape must be conceived in the inseparability of the two, or indeed maintained that we must throw out the distinction between "subject" and "object" before we can begin to think about landscape. For declared inseparability nevertheless implies such a separation. The light

---

4. Ibid. [Translator's note.]
5. Michel Collot, *La Pensée-paysage* (Arles, France: Actes Sud/ENSP, 2011); also in *La Théorie du paysage en France, 1974–1994*, ed. Alain Roger (Seyssel, France: Champ Vallon, 1995), 210.

it sheds is the light generated by the opposition and its tools, even if we later reject said opposition.

This applies notably to the analysis that tends to posit landscape as a "signifying" structure, arguing that all perception, because necessarily selective, is already an interpretation. But does this not still retain landscape for "my own" use, limiting it to my expectation and my projection—in other words, annex it once more to the Subject? Can we show landscape to advantage, and promote its resource, only if we bestow on it a semantic capacity, or at least a semantic predisposition? Perhaps there is no other way to justify the familiar notion that landscape "speaks" to the observer, but nothing proves that the phrase is anything more than a figure of speech. However convenient its repatriation of landscape into everything we know more generally about language, it nonetheless reflects one of the great choices made by European culture: the choice, doubtless arising from religion, that seeks everywhere for an "appeal" to meaning. When will we stop waiting for an Announcement to the world, even through landscape? When will we stop hoping for a "message"?

It becomes plainer still that we will remain within the established conceptual option, no matter how hard we try to deconstruct or contest it, if we take the path of psychoanalysis and approach landscape as a "transition" between subjective space, in which infantine narcissism bathes, and objectivating space, where a child gradually learns to separate (resigns itself to separating?) from itself. The undone separation, because presupposed, remains legitimated. We might otherwise prolong the trial against what Merleau-Ponty—the great source of this rightful suspicion, which has haunted contemporary thought ever since—calls the "over-hastiness" of the grand gesture of separation. But I fear that either approach would lead to an impasse. For one thing, both fail to acknowledge how fertile for *knowledge* the "subject"/"object" fracture and bipartition has been; they fail to acknowledge the unprecedented effect it has had on our mastery of "nature" through science—science constituting, by its own authority, the entirety of "experience" (Kant in his *Prolegomena*: "Thence we shall determine nature as the whole object of all possible experience"[6]). But the gesture that split off the "object" had in fact to be "hasty" if it was to succeed and carry the day, if it was to impose its inventiveness. Had it not swiftly, and perhaps artlessly, taken the initiative to step over any point of resistance or deflection, the gesture would never have been *possible*. It would never have been *dared*.

It therefore seems to me pointless, perhaps, to denounce the subject/object partition for being abrupt, cursory, or even arbitrary. It seems

---

6. From the 1902 edition edited by Paul Carus. The translator's identity is unclear. [Translator's note.]

equally pointless even to take on the task of heading upstream from it, as phenomenology purports to do. The reason is that we now know we cannot lift ourselves by our own bootstraps—*motu proprio*, by our own suspicions or genius—out of the theoretical, atavistic framework within which the partition was invented, the framework that European language built before thought rendered it explicit and doomed us to depend on it. From the inside (of our language) we cannot even judge where or how we are walled in. In truth, we cannot even *imagine* it. It is still another thing to escape the very motivation that led *logically* to the separation.

But there is an observation that we cannot sweep under the rug: Chinese thought has *sidestepped* any such rupture and its categorization. Just consider that translators in the late nineteenth century arrived at a nonsensical pair when, to convey the Western theory of knowledge, they sought to render "subject/object" in Chinese. In the language of the translation they could not shake off or pry apart the implied semantics (even if a new, imported sense could, of course, be grafted onto the semantic pair and adopted through cultural assimilation). What they came up with was "welcoming-welcomed" (主体—客体). The relation, as we can see, is one of hospitality (of "welcoming"), not of neutrality. Here, at last, I see a way to get around what the thought of objectivity has definitively deposited in European language, and a way to rethink *connivance* altogether—without, that is, having to hide it under *knowledge*. Here the Chinese language, because it needn't deconstruct anything, is perhaps better "equipped" to conceive of landscape. So much better that we might conceivably arrive at the following division: European language-thought has *proved able* to promote the theory of knowledge (equipped itself for the task), and Chinese language-thought has all the more effectively *proved able* to clear a place for connivance by not having encumbered itself with the categories of pure knowledge.

5

The famous Tang Dynasty scholar Liu Zongyuan, whom we have already cited, described connivance for us *in Chinese*.[7] He first had to clear the field, mow the rotten grass, and cut down and burn the worm-eaten wood. From the pruning was born a landscape: "Tall trees arose; beautiful bamboos appeared; strange rocks came to light." "It is within all of this that we undertook our contemplation." Whereas a landscape-panorama presents itself *before* an observer's eye, contemplation is here born of the

---

7. Lui Zongyuan, "*Gu mu tan xi xiao qiu ji*," in *Liu Hedong ji*, 472.

landscape's very "milieu" (由其中). And what is it exactly that opens up to contemplation? "The height of the mountain, the flight of the clouds, the precipitous course of the water, the free frolic of the animals." It is a *whole world*, an "exuberant" world, that locally "manifests itself in every sense," "with equal parts artistry and skill," "from the foot of this hill."

This is the moment when a link of connivance is established. A French translation whose quality I do not dispute has impeccably rendered the rest: "I lay down mat and pillow and stretch out. The pure, cold forms speak to my eyes; the murmur of the water speaks to my ear; the void of vast space speaks to my spirit; the silence of the depths speaks to my heart."[8] Note first that I open myself up to landscape when "stretched out," at my leisure, lying on a mat. I do it, that is, when I am most amenable, and not when standing erect like an observer-strategist. More to the point, consider the results of a more precise translation:

> Limpid-cool, forms with the eye are heard;
> murmuring-murmuring, sonorities with the ear are heard;
> at infinity a hollowing-out results: with the spirit it is heard;
> in the depths a calming results: with the heart it is heard.[9]

There is no question of a landscape that "speaks to me," as the first translation reads—and as European language-thought, I admit, leads us so readily to expect. The verb *mou* (謀), essential in strategy, means "plot," "plan," "come to terms with," and "strive to obtain." Here it is repeated as if it were the only possible verb. It bespeaks "complicit understanding," while yet producing no meaning and leading us to suppose no symbolic structure. What we do have, however, is a gradual—or *processual*—slide, by flaring out, into a now endless connivance, with all demarcations effaced. There follows upon the equal and correlated sensorial relation of sight and hearing a deployment that proceeds from itself, meeting with no end and having nothing to direct it. We enter upon a development that opens in the distance as it does in the depths, by immanence. (Need we repeat that it occurs *in* consciousness?) The result, by overflow, is both a "hollowing-out" and a "calming" (although by translating with nouns we once again end up reifying). The process itself is literally, grammatically, the "subject," the only subject there is. The other one, the personal subject, is for its part undone.

---

8. "*Je dispose natte et oreiller, et je m'étends. Les formes pures et froides parlent à mes yeux; le murmure de l'eau parle à mon oreille; le vide de l'espace immense parle à mon esprit; le silence des profondeurs parle à mon cœur.*" [Translator's note.]

9. "*Limpides-fraîches, les formes avec l'œil s'entendent; / murmurantes-murmurantes, les sonorités avec l'oreille s'entendent; / à l'infini il en résulte de l'évidement: avec l'esprit s'entend; / en profondeur il en résulte de l'apaisement: avec le cœur s'entend.*" [Translator's note.]

There is, too, an inverse case: when connivance never comes about. When the world withdraws into itself, recoiling into its beyond, into its own life, and we never accede to landscape: that is, when landscape's resource never opens. This is, at least, the other reading I think we might make of another passage by the same author[10] (although how well can I know how an eighth-century Chinese scholar would feel this internal shift?):

> We sit above the ravine. On all sides bamboos and trees surround us.
> Infinite calm, not a single human being.
> The spirit feels a chill—cold to the bone.
> Calm-desolation filters secretly in.
> It's that the environment is too pure:
> We can linger here no longer.
> I have taken note and gone.

Dug into its world, immaculate as that world is, the landscape here *does not overflow*. It withdraws. Its "limpidity" (清) now becomes inner cold, joined to a sense of dereliction. I no longer feel through it my involvement in the world. The connection to a *primordial kernel* that landscape usually invites me to make never comes to be. No "connivance" advenes.

6

It otherwise remains to be seen how the world, in becoming landscape, brings me into its *tensional field*—how, in Stendhal's comparison, it puts me into resonance with its variation. If I see in this nothing but literary embellishment, then what exactly makes such a phenomenon of "induction" possible? According to Chinese thinkers on painting, the same physical tension pervades both the "actualized form" that I am (*xing*, 形; though "I am" is still too Cartesian) and the form that densifies into landscape (the notion of *tishi*, 体势—as in Tang Dai,[11] for instance). We may limit ourselves to a cursory review of the analogical nomenclatures for which Chinese thought, when routine, has always shown a penchant. In the mountain's constitutive being, the rocks are "bones"; the forests, "garments"; the vegetation, "hairs" and "hair"; the watercourses, "blood vessels"; the clouds and fogs, the "air" of the face; the vapors and mists, the "atmosphere" emanating from the overall person; the temples and belvederes, villages and bridges, "finery" and "jewels"; and so on. Be it known that a mountain has "flanks," "shoulders," a "head," and so forth,

---

10. Liu Zongyuan, "*Gu mu tan xi xiao qui ji*," 473.
11. *Hualun Congkan*, ed. Yu Anlan (Beijing: Zhonggua shuju, 1977), 1:252.

just as I do. At this stage of physical, fixed slackness we have nothing but formal assimilation perceived from without: nothing of interest. What matters, however, is that we have a single dynamic running through our respective actualizations. It is this dynamic that opens the way to communication from the interior, propagating from one to the other, between the "world" and the "self." It allows for a certain tension-setting of the world-becoming-landscape to set me into tension, in unison with that world.

Chinese physics explains this—or, actually, having no need to explain, implies it at all times. The reason that tension-setting spreads from the one to the other is that the "mountain" and the "water" are, like man, a singular individuation of the breath-energy, in continuous propensity, from which the world stems (气). It both condenses (forming the opacity of "bodies") and deploys (forming the "spirit" dimension). If indeed we remove the notion of "matter"—difficult as this admittedly is with our mental habits in Europe (although I believe contemporary physics is no longer in disagreement)—and begin thinking in terms of *process*—materialization on the one hand, animation on the other (the instantiated "soul" is no more present than inert "matter")—then we will understand that *it is no mere image* to say that the mountain "thrusts" or "sits," "leans" or "stands," or even "hangs by its feet." From this point of view, rather, the mountain (or just as easily the water) is specifically said (Tang Zhiqi[12]) to be "equivalent" to my "nature" (性), or the "disposition" affecting the mountain "equivalent" to the "disposition" that affects me (情). It is said that in the name of this "equivalence" there can effectively be a shared *tensional field* between the one and the other.

It is no longer mere rhetorical personification to say that such and such mountain "knows me" as I "know" it (among others,[13] Shu Shu, in the late seventeenth century), that an affinity never to be broken has arisen between us, the mountain "being a lonesome place" and "I myself being a lonesome man," such that for years "I returned every month, and then every day," to this Elephantine mountain, and only a storm could keep me away. A need "to return," a need become vital (everyone is familiar with it), has indeed developed. It falls upon us suddenly, and repeatedly, such that we set off (in Nerval it occurs upon exit from the theater: the return to Valois). Because we read (or say) this under sway of the scheme of *knowledge* and its great theoretical schisms, however, we will still see in it only literary amplification, despite the suasion of experience, *experientia reclamante*. Or, at least, when we say this it seems necessarily, and at best,

---

12. Ibid., 113.
13. "Xiang shan ji," cited in *Les Formes du vent, paysages chinois en prose*, Martine Vallette-Hémery (trans.) (Amiens, France: Le Nyctalope, 1987), 129–31.

like vengeance to compensate for the "deadly" rigor of science and, as *doxa* says, breathe a little "poetry" back into our "disenchanted" world.

I see nothing worse than the supposed healing function of literature, where literature serves as an imaginary escape valve for European reason's venting of steam. But if we turn our minds even slightly from the absolutist realm of *knowledge* (without, of course, failing to acknowledge its own field of pertinence) and restore within ourselves a *dominion of connivance*, we will understand that (it will become coherent that) there arises (should arise) an intimacy between us and places that turn into landscapes, just as it arises, it says herein, with "friends." I am knowing at my desk, but I become connivant once more when I stroll (indeed, this is what "strolling" actually is). Something in the singularization of my vital disposition (情) connects with the singularization of the mountain and brings back to the surface what I have already called my *more primordial involvement with the world*. Yet this remains within the realm of pure phenomenality, and I see no reason to carry it onto the plane of representation *as well*—no reason to explain that the mountain "speaks to me" or "waves to me," that I have made it my "double" and the "mirror image" of my mood, and so forth.

Shitao, the most radical thinker in this regard, developed in the eighteenth century the notion of a *common birth* [*coenfantement*] of the self and the landscape.[14] After all, what gives rise to landscape is precisely the following: it is not that I, the autonomous subject, the subject with initiative (the *knowing* subject), have the landscape at my disposal but, rather, that the landscape has *me* at *its disposal* in equal measure. Each of the two, "self" and "landscape," *brings the other into the world* (*tuo tai*, 脱胎). "Fifty years ago I had not yet given birth to myself in the landscape. Not that I took it to have no value; I merely left it to its own existence." Now, however, "the landscape has me speaking on its behalf." (There is no mention of the landscape's "speaking to me" but of my speaking for it. I serve as its mouthpiece: I express in my painting, with the dash of my brush, the tension-setting that is landscape's.) And henceforth "the landscape is born in me, and I, I am born in the landscape." This is such that "the landscape and I meet in spirit" and "the strokes" (the phenomenal) are thenceforth "transformed." The "encounter" (*yu*, 遇) between the two poles of interaction that are the landscape and me, says Shitao, takes place both at an invisible headwaters and downstream, in its sensible manifestation. Indeed, the peculiarity of landscape as a decisive, revelatory experience is to make us feel in the moment, instantaneously, in the raw, that the dualist rupture is impossible. Landscape does not go beyond the rupture; landscape nullifies it.

---

14. Shitao, *Shan shui*.

7

And so we must, henceforth in a positive light, think through the *primordial coinvolvement* of the "world" and the "self" that rises to the surface in landscape. China holds this to be a sort of primary notion, a foundation that it has never called into question, never dreamed of doubting. On this basis all schools of thought since antiquity have agreed. It is a *common ground* between them. (Thus the Cartesian cogito, which brusquely begins by considering the subject as separate from the world, remains to this day opaque in China, as I have had occasion to observe.) In Zhuangzi, the natural-process thinker, we read, "The world ["Heaven-Earth"] and I were born together" [并生]. "The world and I are co-natural." "All creatures and I myself are but one." In Mencius, the moral thinker, we read, "All creatures are wholly involved in me" (备于我). Nothing more is said, because it is a first principle. These dictums serve as signals, compel emergence, but do not build. (Would it end up destroying them to undertake any "building"?) But the world's involvement in me—an involvement normally paralyzed, engulfed, and forgotten—has in return an effect of its own: the involvement is what reappears upon our encounter with landscape and translates to *connivance*.

China has thought out a solidarity between the self and the world in its most concrete form. It has so thoroughly erased the boundary between the human and the nonhuman as to have shaken our "humanism." Wary though I am of its current ideological use in China—where it is seen as foundational to ecology and thus (let us not mince words) as countering, or substituting for, the notion of human rights—we must acknowledge that some such concern, some such care for the world, prepared the way for landscape. We find a notable expression of this in the tradition of Mencius by the great sixteenth-century thinker Wang Yangming[15] (whose text is now held up by the New Confucianism as a manifesto for the planet's well-being). Time and again he establishes not only that all human beings are a single being, and that whosoever separates them by physical constitution and distinguishes between "you" and "me" is a "good-for-nothing," obliterating the spontaneous impulse of his nature, but also that the "intolerable sensation" we feel when any member of humanity is suddenly imperiled (when a child is about to fall into well, to take Mencius's example) is the same reaction we feel when we make animals suffer, or cause the deterioration of plants, or even destroy "tiles" and "stones," though these have neither consciousness nor feeling or life. The human being, he concludes, rooted as he is in the great Process of natural regulation, and feeling his "injunction" (天命), cannot help but find within himself the "clear light" of this universal sympathy.

---

15. Wang Yangming, *"Daxuewen,"* in *Wang Wencheng Gong quanshu*, chap. 26.

This constitutes a "foundation"—nonontological, it is true—for landscape thought and the *connivance* revealed through it. It removes from within the world's process the demarcation not just between the human and the nonhuman, or interiority and physicality, but also between what corresponds to "things" and what corresponds to "spirit." Recall that "thing" is here called "east-west" and aptly symbolizes the tension-by-polarity that "animates" all "reality." The entire world, within and without us, is, Chinese thought tells us, made of interactions ("inter-incitements," 相感) that link up, respond to one another, and echo indefinitely. It is incumbent on man to carry within him the awareness of said interactions. Is there any other "reality"? It is these interactions that endlessly and without limit weave together the landscape, the great correlation of "mountains" and "waters," and I find that I partake in its slightest advent. The physicality of the world touches me from one end of its development to the other. I am part of that physicality.

The garden, being removed from the world and walled in, has served to separate man from nature (in the Bible and the Koran), whereas landscape has done the reverse. The limitless tensions that landscape opens up have no truck with any separation or secession in principle. In these tensions the human perceives a bottomless well of existence. Within the integration the human finds its "element" to be sufficient. Such is the "Revelation," or what I will call the *temptation*, of landscape. Petrarch, if indeed he wished to root himself in faith and remain loyal to God, was right to turn away from the landscape he discovered from the summit of Mount Ventoux, as he reports in his epistolary account, where all is still symbolic: "I was cross with myself for continuing to admire terrestrial realities" (*quod nunc etiam terrestria mirarer*), for "only the spirit"—that is, the spirit detached from the world—"is fit for admiration."

8

I do not know quite what to call it. Its few square meters can accommodate several people. Its roof of varnished tiles and furring strip provides shelter from the sun and the rain. When not circular it is often hexagonal or octagonal, and thus favors no single perspective, inviting you instead to turn every which way. Columns, fundamental to the architecture, leave it wide open to the landscape. Here you do not stand *before* the landscape, your gaze plunging to the horizon, but are *immersed* in it. It is not a belvedere, because you do not repair to it merely for the "lovely view." In fact, it rarely sits atop a mountain but, more often, about halfway down, and might as easily lodge in a hollow as rest on an outcrop. You spot it from afar, in a tangle of vegetation, and then chance upon it as you round a bend in the path and find it most convenient for a halt. Nor is it a house where you might dwell. It lacks both furnishings and amenities, and is not closed. Its common name in Chinese is *ting* (亭); in translation, "kiosk."

For a long time I wondered why these red- or ocher-roofed kiosks were built. They pepper the landscape of the Far East, and I know of no equivalent structures in Europe. What was their purpose? To contrast the constructed and the natural? To set geometry into the landscape? To cultivate art here and there in nature's midst? Finally, after reading about them in the beautiful prose of great Chinese scholars, I came to an obvious conclusion. The kiosks are there so that we can *enter into connivance* with the landscape. A kiosk is the opposite of a toposcope, or of a "view" shown on a map. With either of those we pause to view the plain from the optimal perspective, diligently identify places by name, and quickly set off, having seen the "view." ("Seen it!" as tourists famously say.) A kiosk provides rest and shelter, but it also allows us to partake as *flâneurs*. There we can take tea, go in and out, and relax. We can play, or recite poetry. We can spend some time, and even forget time altogether.

Because we can spend hours there, we can sense from within a kiosk the silent transformations of the daylight and the weather. Because a kiosk is open year round, we can experience the turn of the seasons. At a kiosk we listen as much as we look. A strident cry breaks the steady rustle of branches in the wind. A cloud's shadow flits past on the ground. We experience the landscape in its ever-shifting nuance. We take our fill of landscape as we take our fill of what brings to light for us what the world is. This is why kiosks are built. They are built specifically for this pleasure, but the pleasure itself amounts to Revelation. We go to a kiosk and take our rest there in order to reach a discreet understanding, which both develops as the hours go by and is at the same time final. No other understanding is to be expected. In a kiosk we are removed from the ordinary world, from plans and ambitions, and from objectives and obligations. We "realize"—though of course there is no need to say "what" we realize. Nothing is forced, nothing imposed. In particular, there is no ecstasy. But there is diffuse imbuing and decantation: simply because we have departed from our former *knowing* state and entered into *connivance*.

No kiosk goes nameless. The one I have in mind was called Kiosk of the Drunken Old Man (in Ouyang Xiu, eleventh century[16]). The governor (Ouyang Xiu himself) would go there to drink with his guests, and the merest sip would get him drunk. "Sense," however, "is not to be found in wine." It "resides" in the landscape or, better yet, "in the interspace between the mountains and the waters"—*(V)ivre de paysage*, that is, to live

---

16. Ouyang Xiu, "*Zui weng ting ji*."

off (*vivre de*) / be drunk on (*ivre de*) landscape. This is a drunkenness that, once again, becomes intelligible through the nondistinction of the literal from the figurative. "We accede to the joy of mountains and waters in spirit," it is said, "at the same time as we place it in wine." It is *between*, not before. "The fog lifts with the rise of the sun" or "the ravines darken with the return of the clouds": these are transformations "between the mountains." We go there in the morning, come back in the evening. "The scene is never the same," but "contentment never runs dry."

From without comes the alternating rhythm of the great clockwork of the world: between those "with burdens, singing on the road" and those "who rest in the shade of the trees," and between "hunched old-timers" and "little children in arms." Life's "to-and-fro" never ceases. To the inside the mountain flats jut and commingle artlessly, and lutes and flutes are done without. At darts "every toss is a bull's-eye"; at chess "everyone wins." Invitations to drink come casually from all sides. All biases fade away; all privileges are lifted. In the kiosk we forget all distinctions of order, all distinctions between things, all criteria and qualifications, and all losses and victories. Success and failure are no more, and everything happens at the right time just as it is. We attain connivance at a kiosk because there we accede to a worldly intelligence that *no longer excludes*.

The kiosk's function—though without fanfare, without mystique or "communion"—is to *undo the separation*. Within it we are at once in- and outdoors, exposed and sheltered. The "Kiosk of the Flying Spring" evoked by Yuan Mei (in the eighteenth century)[17] keeps the waterfall within earshot even with the windows closed, just as it allows droplets to enter with the windows open. One can do one or the other: "sit or lie, or leave one's legs nonchalantly parted, or remain stretched out supine, head turned skyward"; or else one can "set down brush and inkstone," and "brew and savor tea." One can hear the one and the other: "the sound of the water, the sound of chessmen, the sound of pines, the sound of birds," all of which "blends together in concert." To this, moreover, we add the psalmody of recited poems. Also, the "music of the human world" (*renlai*, 人籟) and the music emitted of its own accord everywhere in nature (*tianlai*, 天籟) are "united in a single transformation" and can no longer be discerned. "Transitive" action (as the *Zhuangzhi* teaches) is no longer distinguishable from the spontaneous. The kiosk is the place where the disjunction is erased, where relations of causality and assignation—in short, all of the building blocks of *knowledge*—lose their prerogative. By restoring *connivance*, however, the kiosk makes immanence audible to the ear, and thereby grants entry to landscape.

---

17. Yuan Mei, "*Xia jiang shi fei quan ting ji.*"

Strolling along and seeking to rest, Su Dongpo happens upon the "Kiosk of Wind in the Pines," which he spots amid the treetops. "How shall I reach it?"[18] he asks, and wonders at length. Then, suddenly, "Where in all this *interspace* would I not find such a place to rest?" Now I was "like a hooked fish that finds itself suddenly free." Once you have understood this, concludes Su Dongpo, nothing can prevent you from "allowing the most perfect calm to grow within you"—not even the height of battle, when the drums are pounding like thunder and "you are as sure to be killed by the enemy if you advance as to face a death penalty if you retreat." And thus we needn't bother even to distinguish "kiosk" from "nonkiosk," the spot where a kiosk stands from a spot where none is to be found. In other words, we needn't pretend to undertake its assignation and seek it in its rightful place; we needn't want to get there or to set the objective, which we attain or not. The "kiosk" exists wherever I surrender to connivance and let things come to me—though I am no longer "me," no longer my *ego*. This is what it means to "realize." The kiosk is thenceforth in the "interspace." That is, it has no location of its own, no "property." It is everywhere in the *interspace*-landscape, once one knows how to establish it, as in like manner the landscape is anywhere I can find—anywhere I know how to find—a "kiosk."

---

18. Su Dongpo, "*Ji you song feng ting.*"

Epilogue

Anyone who has seen a painting by a Chinese scholar or read a few poems by a Jin or a Tang has to some extent already perceived this. It is evident at the slightest encounter, even in passing, with China's traditional culture. And yet the sinologist, after decades of patient circling, cannot always manage to express it—or perhaps even to conceive of it. For how do you go about undoing your own language, unfolding your reasons, and venturing far enough upstream just to be able to say "mountain(s)-water(s)" in Chinese? How do you venture far enough to name the "mountain" and by the same token the "water," or to pair the "wind" with the "light"? How do you fully convey what it is that, in its deployment, gives rise to world-ness, and then feel no need to posit and yearn for a Beyond?

And we do this with no need for further construction or derivation, only for pairing. Because landscape, as Chinese tells us, is to be found in the interspace, and therefore escapes the philosophy of Being, of peculiarity, and of assignation. It follows, moreover, that it escapes the philosophy of model-making and ideality, as it does any shift to another plane. By putting into play the various correlations that weave it together in the first place, Chinese thought has never needed to erect an architecture of thought. It classifies, establishes typologies, and adjoins into pairs, but it never erects. This, among other things, is why landscape thought has left Chinese thought without theoretical or political edification: China has devised learning, not Science; it has thought through power, not the city-state. Thus Chinese thought lacks an idea of Liberty (and therefore of Truth) that is free of the world's conditions and stands absolute, outside the world—an idea one could use as a guide, in whose name one could struggle, criticize, look to the future, and advance history. Landscape thought has retracted other possibilities; it too comes at a cost.

But today, when the Subject no longer needs introduction or promotion in isolation from a "self," as it did in philosophy's heroic era, we will learn from landscape to rethink our relation to the world. This is why landscape thought is worth our while to develop. We must escape the dilemma that contemporary ideology tends to drive us toward, where we either treat the world mechanically (decapitate it, as machine logic and the imperative to generate a yield would have us do) or else yearn for a paradise lost, dream nostalgically of a "symbiosis" with the world, bring the perennial suit against science and technics, and invoke Nature and Life (our hypostatic "green" and "organic") as our guarantor and savior. But we tire of the new mythology du jour, the great contemporary incantation and prophecy that would have us revert to the bosom and crawl penitently back into the womb.

Landscape thought, meanwhile, leads us to rediscover our more primordial involvement in the world. It takes us beneath the underpinnings of reason but occasions no slide into irrationalism. It leads us to spring the Subject from its solipsistic enclosure but makes it a vassal to no new lord and does not alienate it. Because it is a "resource," landscape is, as the Chinese say, open to "savoring," and is even a vehicle for Revelation, like an inexhaustible well, but imposes no order peculiar to it and conveys no Message. We can live off and draw from landscape endlessly, but we can also "bypass" its resource. It is possible to have never frequented a landscape in one's life. Thus landscape harkens back reciprocally to the Subject's availability, calling on and promoting it. We must now conceive of an ethics of availability, through the unfencing of a "self." This is to complement—not go beyond—the ethics of Liberty, which seeks the emancipation of a "self."

It behooves us to develop landscape thought, furthermore, insofar as it will allow us to rearticulate some of our contradictions, notably those—atavistic in philosophy—of immanence and transcendence: another frozen pair to go along with subject and object. Rather than have us think of them as rivals, landscape leads us to conceive of a transcendence that decants from the physical and by the same token remains physically processual. It opens the way to a beyond only by "clearing out and opening up [*dégagement*]." By calling it "immanent to the world" we would already be losing it, because once again we would be making the World into an instance of transcendence. Thus we would no longer need to posit an Elsewhere as a Beyond "cut off" from the world and serving as an alibi.

Today, moreover, now that things have reached a global scale, landscape's virtue in the face of such abstract ubiquity lies in its power of relocation: not through illusory withdrawal into some compensatory and picturesque particularism but through the reinstatement of the Singular. If what gives rise to landscape is an encompassing of the world's entirety, albeit in a single way, then the locality itself, in its ceaseless incitement to interaction and communication, is global. It is thus of no importance whether a landscape is made of streets or valleys, urban districts or forests. We will not be leaving our mega-cities as once we repaired to the countryside. What matters is the advent of multiple polarities that set the world in tension and rescue it from impending uniformity, which will doom it to boredom by atony before relegating it to indifference. Landscape's virtue is that it invites discovery and encounter, until the Exterior transforms into "the innermost interior" (deeper than our interior designated as such) and becomes intimate, and until the Exterior takes that "region in which to live," invoked by Mallarmé as well as Plato, and repatriates it such that it becomes the here.

Index

abstraction, x, 3, 6–8, 11, 18, 22, 32, 35, 44, 63, 79, 86, 99, 106, 124
accession, 5, 7, 12, 30, 51, 59, 65–66, 114, 120
activation, 24, 38–39, 54, 58, 77, 79, 81, 84, 88, 92–94; vs. order, 71
actualizing form, 31
adequation, 3n4, 28, 68
adherence/adhesion, 11, 66, 84, 105–6. *See also* dis-adherence
adret and ubac, 21, 60, 92
advent, 3, 5, 8n8, 21, 28, 37, 45, 47, 49, 51, 57, 66, 69, 81, 100, 114, 118, 125
the affectual, ix, 9, 44, 53, 56; vs. affect, 43–44; muting by diversity, 43; vs. the perceptual, 41–46, 49–51, 56; with respect to behavior and morality, 44; with respect to emotion, 44; with respect to nature-emotion, 49
Âge Classique, 101
Alberti, Leon Battista, 33–36, 33n8, 91
alchemy, 54, 62
Altmann, Johann Georg, 74
Analects, 22, 46, 46n4
analysis vs. synthesis, 19
Aristotle, 7–8, 19, 85

artialization, 71, 76, 78, 80, 84
the aspectual, 7, 11–12, 19, 22, 39, 89
assemblage, 9, 9n10, 13, 68, 71, 91–92, 99, 108
assignation, 8–9, 8n8, 11, 36, 44, 47, 63, 89, 120–21, 123
atony, 77, 79, 88, 100, 125. *See also* the intensive vs. the atonic
Augustine, 8, 59
aura, 54–56, 58, 61–66, 84, 98, 100, 109

Baudelaire, Charles, 9, 11, 68
Beaubourg, 81
beauty, 3, 9, 11, 25, 32, 39, 42–43, 68, 73–78, 88, 90, 102, 112, 119; vs. the sublime, 45, 72
becoming, 84, 94. *See also* being, vs. becoming
being, xi, 6, 21, 28, 31–32, 38, 47, 52, 54, 56, 62–63, 65, 90, 98, 123; vs. becoming, 56, 69; vs. nonbeing, 94–95; with respect to eternity, identity, and immortality, 62
"being there" (*Dasein*), 86, 98
Benjamin, Walter, 62
Bergson, Henri, 42, 42n2
Berque, Augustin, 69, 100

Index

the beyond, ix, 7, 31, 42, 45, 63, 84–85, 94, 96, 98–100, 103, 114, 116, 123–24
the Bible, x, 118
bigger soul (Bergson), 42, 42n2
blandness, 63. *See also* savoring
blurring, 11, 24, 35, 41, 63, 71, 98
Borges, Jorge Luis, 31
Boudin, Eugène, 87
breadth, 36, 42, 46, 58, 74, 92–93
breath-energy (*qi*), 29–30, 37–38, 46, 54, 57, 60, 63–64, 70, 115. *See also* soaring (*l'essor*)
Buddhism, 51, 59–60, 65–66

Callias, 85
capacity, 6–7, 31–32, 38, 43–44, 49, 55, 71, 107, 109, 111
Centre Pompidou. *See* Beaubourg
Cézanne, Paul, 30, 34
chantier, x, xn6, 4n6
The Charterhouse of Parma, 102, 108, 114
Chenet-Faugeras, Françoise, 68, 68n2, 71
chi. *See* breath-energy (*qi*)
Church fathers, 88
citizenship, 19, 38
Civiale, Aimé, 74
"Claire de lune," 22, 22n4
Claudel, Paul, 106, 106n1
clearing out and opening up (*dégagement*), 56, 58, 60, 65–66, 70, 74, 100, 124
the closed vs. the open, 78, 83n1, 94, 119. *See also* garden
coherence, 1, 17, 20–21, 23, 28–29, 92, 100–1, 105
coincidence. *See* de-coincidence vs. coincidence
Collot, Michel, 98, 110, 110n5
the common, 17–18, 17n2, 85
communion (with nature), 105, 108, 120
comparison, ix, 21, 101, 106, 108, 114
composition, ix, 2–3, 19–20, 22, 33–34, 67–68, 70–71, 79, 81, 91, 93; com-position (European notion etymologically revealed), 19; decomposition, 49
compossibility, 30–32, 36, 74
com-prehension (European notion etymologically revealed), 19
co-naissance, 106, 106n1
Confessions (Augustine), 59
Confucius, 22, 46, 46n4, 117
connivance, x, 103, 105–21; as the consequence of involvement, 117; in poetry, 107; as revealed by landscape-thought, 118; return to, 109; vs. knowledge, 106–7, 112, 116, 119
consciousness, 51, 85, 105, 113, 117
conservation (American movement), 5, 75. *See also* environment
consistency, 28–29, 31–32, 34, 46–49, 81, 92, 95, 110
contemplation, 13, 25, 72, 96, 112–13
Corot, Jean-Baptiste-Camille, 80
correlation, ix, 11, 14–15, 18–20, 24, 26, 29–30, 32–33, 36, 39, 41, 46, 48–52, 55–58, 66, 68, 70, 79, 81–82, 91, 118, 123; in acupuncture, 20; in magnetism, 20; of the prince and the people, 20
Cubism, 63
Curiosités esthétiques, 68, 68n1
cutoff, 1–14, 15–16, 19, 24, 35, 43, 61, 67, 75–76, 94–95, 110, 124; in Plato, 61

Dasein / da sein, 22, 86
de-coincidence vs. coincidence, 3n4
dehiscence, 99
Delimitation: as the path of knowledge, 96; Greek tendency toward, 95; in the notion of landscape, 95; of the horizon, ix, 5, 16, 24; vs. effacement, 97
Demiéville, Paul, 68
density, 47, 80, 82, 92
deployment, x, xn5, 1, 1n1, 11–12, 16, 21, 24, 30–34, 36–38, 47, 54–55, 57, 61–62, 64–66, 68, 77, 84, 89, 92, 94–95, 98, 100, 113, 115, 123

Descartes, René, 4, 6, 19, 88, 105–6, 114, 117
detour, 4, 4n5, 55
Dictionnaire de Trévoux, 90, 90n7
dis-adherence, 99. See also adherence/adhesion
diversity, 32, 43, 66, 70, 75, 88, 92
divide (écart), ix, ixn1, xn2, 4, 5n7, 8n8, 11, 13, 17–18, 17n2, 21, 24–25, 27, 31, 41n1, 71–72, 81, 84, 87–89, 92, 95
Du Fu, 68
Dürer, Albrecht, 28
dwelling, x, 25, 37, 40, 50, 55–56, 74, 78, 91, 93, 103, 119; vs. crossing, 39–40

east-west (*dong xi*), 20–21, 25, 118
écart. See divide
effacement, 84, 97. See also Delimitation, vs. effacement
effect of consciousness (Bewusstseinseffekt), 69
ego, 75, 121
Eiffel Tower, 81
encounter, 8n8, 33, 42, 51–52, 60, 85–86, 88, 99, 102, 107, 109–10, 116–17, 123, 125
Enlightenment, 101n25, 106
environment, x, 24, 37, 52, 75–76, 114
Eros, 78
essence, 8, 21, 28, 32, 36, 47, 63, 87, 89–90. See also quintessence
evocation, 12, 44, 50, 57, 59, 62, 78, 86–87, 97, 101–2, 120
existence, ix, xi, 21, 31, 48, 60, 62, 66, 72, 81, 83–86, 92, 116, 118, 121. See also singularity/singularization
Existentialism, 85
eyesore, 80–81

fecundity, 17, 47
flâneur. See roaming (or wandering)
flaring, 55–57, 59, 61, 94, 97, 99–100, 113
fold, xn5, 1, 1n1, 5, 9, 18, 21–24, 36, 45, 55, 56n1, 70, 77, 83, 83n1, 85, 90–91, 93–96, 123

Fontenell, Bernard Le Bovier de, 89, 89n6
form-actualization (*xing*), 30–32
form-tension, 64, 70
Foucault, Michel, 31
Freud, Sigmund, 69
Frodsham, J. D., 23, 23n6
Furetière, Antoine, 2, 90, 90n7

Galen, 6
garden: French vs. Chinese, 79; garden-thought, x, 118. See also landscape, vs. garden
gaze, ix, 12–14, 18, 24–26, 74, 96, 102–3, 118
Genesis, 54
geometry, ix, 9, 19, 71, 79–80, 95, 101, 119
Gu Kaizhi, 59
Guo Feng, 47, 47n5
Guo Xi, 30, 30n6, 32–39, 34n10, 64, 64n8, 86, 86n2, 96

Haller, Albrecht von, 72
Han Dynasty, 100
Hegel, Wilhelm Friedrich, 85; vs. Kierkegaard, 85
Heraclitus, 71
horizon, 5–7, 75, 94, 98, 108, 110; as a mistranslation from Chinese, 95–97
Hugo, Victor, 9
Human, All Too Human. See "The Wanderer and His Shadow"

I-Ching, 21, 47
identity, 28, 64; with respect to being, eternity, and immortality, 62
imbuing (*prégnance*), 8, 8n8, 40, 48, 63, 65
immortality: with respect to being, eternity, and identity, 62
Impressionism, 34, 87
India, x
induction, 43, 45, 50, 114
infinity, 57
integration, 71, 81
intensification, 63, 68–69, 71, 74

the intensive vs. the atonic, 77
interspace, 41–42, 41n1, 47, 65, 72, 84, 89, 121
the intimate, xi, xin7, 9, 41, 107
Islam, x, 118

Jin Dynasty, 123
Julie, or the New Heloise, 67, 90–91, 90n8, 91n10, 93, 93n11

kalos. *See tonos* vs. *kalos*
Kant, Emmanuel, 39, 44–45, 111
Kierkegaard, Søren, 85. *See also* Hegel, Wilhelm Friedrich
kiosk (*ting*), 118–21
Koran, 118

Lacoste, Yves, 13
Lamartine, Alphonse de, 49, 49n8
landscape: as assemblage, 68; common birth (*co-enfantement*) of with the self, 116; as a corner of the world, ix, 18, 85, 99; as correlation, 68; as our double (in Nietzsche's sense), 110; durativity of, 43; as an effect, 69;European notion of, 9; as a European term, 2, 67; to be experienced, or lived, 37, 39; flaring-out of, 59, 61; vs. garden, x, 71, 78–79, 94, 118; as a link, 107, 109; as a locus of exchange, 40, 50; and metaphysics, 60–61; vs. natural surroundings (in Nietzsche's sense), 109; in poetry, 22, 62; as polarity, 50; as a process, 49–50, 95; promotion of, 68; as tension-setting, 101; vs. view, 10–12, 44, 73, 84; world-ness as condition of, 84, 108, 113, 125
landscape-ment, 69, 73, 81, 90
landscape-thought, x, 1–2, 4–6, 8, 18, 33, 41, 45, 59, 61, 76, 89, 95, 100, 109
Laozi, 18, 60
liberty, xi, 9, 39, 45, 123–24
Life of Henri Beyle, 43, 43n3, 109
Littré dictionary, 6
Liu Xie, 47n5, 100, 100n24

Liu Zongyuan, 93, 93n12, 112, 112n7, 114, 114n10
living (*vivre*), x–xi, xn3, 1n1, 4n6, 16n1, 24, 26, 27–40, 67–69, 71–72, 74–6, 79, 84, 93–94, 100, 102, 106, 109–10
longevity vs. eternity, 38
looking, ix–x, 2, 7, 10, 12–13, 15, 17, 25, 31, 34–5, 39–40, 70, 72, 74, 79, 102, 119; as a verb in Chinese, 25–26; with vs. through the eyes, 13
Lorrain, Claude, 3

magnetism, 20, 45, 50. *See also* correlation, in magnetism
Mallarmé, Stéphane, 125
meaning, 7, 23, 32n7, 47, 100, 113; appeal to, 111
melting, 61, 63, 66, 95, 97; as an obstacle to dualism, 66. *See also* spirit
Mencius, 117
Merleau-Ponty, Maurice, 111
Mestre, 81
metaphysics, 14, 31–32, 37, 53, 57, 60, 64, 71, 77–78, 93, 95; gesture of, 76, 111
Metaphysics (Aristotle), 7
Mi Fu, 29, 29n4
"Milly ou la terre natale," 49, 49n8
mimesis, 39
mitage, 81–82
mobilization/mobilism, 36–39, 44, 65, 77; immobilization, 36, 98
models/model-making, 55, 71, 79, 123
Modernism, 81
Montaigne, Michel de, 71n5
Montesquieu, 72
mood, 44, 77, 116
"mountain(s)-water(s)" (*shan shui*), 15–26, 27, 29, 33, 39, 46, 48, 51, 57, 59, 70, 118, 123. *See also* symbol(ism)

negative and the ugly, championing of, 76
Nerval, Gérard de, 115
the new, xn6

New Confucianism, 117
Nietzsche, Friedrich, 71, 71n4, 109, 109n3
the nonhuman, 42, 117–18
Notre Dame de Paris, 10–11, 74
nourishment, 37, 62

the object, 4, 8, 10–12, 34, 38–39, 42, 54, 100, 106;vetymology of, 10; European invention of, 9; landscape as, 86, 110; nature as, 8, 106; objectivation of knowledge, 8, 50, 53; space as, 111. *See also* subject-object relation
objectivity, 8–9, 33, 45–46, 99, 101, 105, 107, 112
observer, ix–x, 2–5, 7, 9, 12–13, 15–16, 22, 25, 33, 36, 42, 45, 50, 67–68, 75, 90, 94, 100–1, 111–13
ontology, 8, 32, 36, 47, 63, 89–90, 98, 100
the open. *See* the closed vs. the open
Ouyang Xiu, 119, 119n16
overflow/spill-over, 3, 12, 31–32, 56, 69, 84, 97–98, 113–14. *See also* symbol(ism)

pairing: in the Chinese language, 16, 18–25, 27, 29–30, 32, 36, 46, 48–49, 64, 91–92, 112, 123; in landscape, 44; in Wang Wei, 91–92; in the Western thought, 90, 108, 124
parataxis, 19, 30
part-whole relation, 5–7, 16, 18–19, 71, 108
Patinir, Joachim, 2, 28
paysage. *See* landscape
La Pensée paysage, 110, 110n5
the perceived, 6, 41–42; vs. the perceptible, 44
the perceptual, 41; vs. the affectual; vs. the perceived, 44; with respect to wind-light, 49. *See also* the affectual
perspective, 33–35
Petrarch, ix, 59, 118
phenomenality, 43, 45, 49, 51–52, 105, 116

phenomenology, 32, 112
photography, 73–74
physics. *See* science
Plato, 13–14, 19, 31, 37, 49, 61, 71, 77–78, 95, 125
pleasure, 22, 39, 42–43, 67, 71, 76, 79, 87, 90, 110, 119
Plotinus, 14
Plutarch, 78
poikilia, 88
point of view. *See* vantage point
polarity, 11, 14, 16, 20–22, 26, 29–30, 36, 38, 41, 49–50, 61, 69, 72, 77, 79, 81–82, 84, 90–92, 97, 118, 125
politics, 19–20, 22, 38, 48, 58, 75, 100, 123
Pontaventism, 87, 87n4
Pont de Sully, 10
possibility, 10, 12–13, 17, 31–32, 36, 38, 44–45, 49, 54–56, 56n1, 77, 89, 93, 98–99, 101, 111, 114, 124; impossibility, 29, 36, 47, 87, 99, 116
potential, 24, 31, 69, 72, 84; vs. act, 69
Poussin, Nicolas, 3
Primitivism, 87
primordial coinvolvement of the "world" and the "self," 117
process, 16n1, 28–29, 35, 45, 50, 54, 57–58, 64, 66, 79, 90, 95, 113, 115, 117–18, 124
Prolegomena, 111, 111n6
promotion, x–xi, xn4, 7–9, 19–20, 29, 34, 38, 40, 48, 56, 60, 62–63, 67–69, 72, 76–78, 83, 85, 89–90, 92, 94, 105, 107–8, 111–12, 124
Proust, Marcel, 109
psychoanalysis, 111

quintessence, 54–55. *See also* essence

Ravier, François-Auguste, 3
receptivity, 12, 44, 47
The Red and the Black, 11–12, 102
reification, 29, 62, 98, 113
remove, ix, 11, 34–36, 42, 83–103; three modes of, 34–36
Renaissance, x, 5, 8, 16, 34, 73, 80, 100

renewal, 17, 22, 30, 38, 84, 92
representation, x, 3, 7, 10, 17, 33, 39, 99, 101, 116
resemblance, 3, 11, 28–29
resource, x–xi, xn2, 4–5, 7–8, 11, 17, 31, 37n14, 39, 43–44, 49, 54–56, 67, 70, 84, 111, 114, 124
revelation, 54, 56–57, 59, 65, 108, 116, 118–19, 124
revitalization, 37–38. *See also* resource
roaming (or wandering), 10–11, 14, 23, 40, 74, 79, 119; *flâneur*, 119; processual, 35
Robert dictionary, 2, 5, 12
rocks and clouds, 29–30
Roger, Alain, 68n2, 71–74, 71n5, 73n7, 76, 110n5
Romanticism, 3, 9, 42, 50, 76, 86, 105, 108, 110
Rousseau, Jean-Jacques, 67, 72, 90–91, 90n8, 91n10, 93, 93n11, 102

Saint-Simon, 79
salience, 83
savoring, 66, 96, 100, 120, 124. *See also* blandness
scholasticism, 85
science, 5, 54–55, 57, 68, 72, 85, 100–1, 105–7, 111, 116, 123–24; Chinese physics, 20, 115; physics, 19, 45, 53, 101, 105, 115
scientific objectivity. *See* objectivity
"Secret Recipe for Mountains and Water," 91, 97
self-subject, 18, 23, 45, 49–50, 108, 110, 124
self-sufficiency, xi, 3n4, 110. *See also* de-coincidence vs. coincidence
Sérusier, Paul, 87
Seven Wonders of the World, 74
Shishuo Xinyu, 48, 48n7
Shitao, 64, 70, 70n3, 116, 116n14
Shu Shu, 115
Sikong Tu, 63, 63n7
singularity/singularization, ix, 4, 7, 18–19, 34, 44, 48, 55, 61, 69, 83–103, 107–9, 115–16, 125; of existence, 84–85; vs. the extraordinary, 84; vs. extremity, 84; vs. peculiarity, 84
slack (*l'étale*), 4n6, 16n1, 62, 74, 77, 86, 99, 115. *See also* soaring (*l'essor*)
soaring (*l'essor*), xn4, 4n6, 16, 16n1, 24, 29–30, 38, 47, 57, 59–62, 64, 70, 80–82, 99. *See also* slack (*l'étale*); as breath-energy (*qi*), 57
Socrates, 85
spectacle, ix, 9, 18, 43–44, 59, 68, 74, 90
spectator, 39; exteriority of, 9
spill-over. *See* overflow/spill-over
Spinoza, Baruch, 45
spirit, ix, 9, 29, 31, 52, 53–66, 70, 98, 109, 113–16, 118, 120; issuing from the physical, 56; and melting, 61; as a process, 54
Spiritualism, 52, 53, 87
Standard Histories, 58
Stein, Alfred R., 79, 79n9
Stendhal, 11–12, 43, 43n3, 68, 102–3, 108–9, 114
Stoicism, 88
strategy, 4, 100, 113. *See also* detour
the structural, 5, 19, 38, 47, 69, 71, 80–81, 90, 111, 113, 119
the Subject, xi, 5–6, 8–10, 14, 16, 18, 23, 25, 33, 36, 41–42, 44–45, 49–50, 52–53, 66, 68, 75, 77, 79, 84, 86, 94, 96, 100–2, 105, 107–13, 116–17, 124; monopoly of, 14. *See also* self-subject
subjectivist surplus, 53. *See also* bigger soul (Bergson)
subjectivity, 9, 44–45, 52, 66, 84, 107, 111
subject-object relation, 5, 8, 10, 14, 61–62, 66, 110–12, 124; translation into Chinese, 111
substance, 20, 52, 54, 61–62, 73
substantialist bias (of the West), 33, 61
substantiation, 47, 56, 64
Su Dongpo, 28, 121, 121n18
Sully-Morland office building, 81
Sumplêrôsis, 88

symbol(ism), 7, 93, 99, 113, 118; de-symbolization/secularization of landscape, 28; vs. going-beyond, 98; as idealization of landscape, 78; as killer of landscape, 78; in mountain(s)-water(s), 22; vs. overflow, 98; of places, 8

Le Talisman, 87
Tang Dai, 29, 29n3, 114, 114n11
Tang Dynasty, 91, 93, 112, 123
Tang Zhiqi, 115, 115n12
Taoism, 37, 58, 61, 65, 100
tension, ix, 11–12, 14, 16, 18, 20–26, 29–31, 37, 39, 51, 58–60, 64, 66, 67–82, 84, 86, 88–94, 100–2, 107–9, 114–16, 118, 125; as a philosophical concept, 69; by polarity, 118; tensional field, 72, 80, 108, 114; world-tension, 60
Theaetetus, 13
thing-ness, ix, 10, 20–21, 25, 31–33, 35, 47, 54–55, 58–60, 62, 69, 80, 83, 85, 90, 96, 98–99, 105, 107, 118
tonos vs. *kalos*, 77–78
transcendence, 38, 55–56, 59–62, 78–79, 84, 99, 124
traversing, 22–24, 39–40, 47, 62, 64–65. See also dwelling
Treatise on Landscape (Guo Xi), 37, 37n13
Très riches heures du Duc de Berry, 27
truth, 45, 73, 103; absence of in Buddhism, 66; absence of in Chinese painting, 35, 123; absence of in the concept of spirit, 54; absence of in Guo Xi's quest, 38–39; vs. the good, 45; in metaphysics, 37; in perspective, 33–35; in Platonism, 95; in representation, 10
Turner, Joseph Mallord William, 3
Two Sources of Morality and Religion, 42, 42n2

ubac. See adret and ubac
unfolding. See fold
the unthought-of, 4, 21

vagueness, 36, 44, 63, 75, 84, 94, 97
vantage point (point of view/viewpoint), ix, 5, 7, 9, 13, 16, 18, 21, 23, 25, 33–34, 44, 68, 79
variation, 24, 31, 47, 74, 80, 83–103, 106, 114
Vasari, Giorgio, 29
Verlaine, Paul, 22, 22n4
view, 1–14, 15, 18, 43–44, 68, 72–74, 84–85, 90, 92, 94, 96, 118–19; monopolizing view, 74. See also vision, monopoly of
vis-à-vis, 5, 5n7, 16, 20, 23, 48, 65, 91, 102. See also *divide* (écart)
vision, 5, 7–8, 10, 12, 25, 39, 68, 76, 97; and conquest, 101; and the horizon, 98; monopoly of, 5, 11, 16; and the perception of landscape, 12, 69, 75; primacy of, 44; vision-conception, 71
vitality, 18, 29–30, 32, 37–39, 58, 69, 70, 79–80, 84, 88, 92–94, 105–6, 109, 115–16
Vitruvius, 2
Voltaire, 11

"The Wanderer and His Shadow" (*Human, All Too Human*), 71, 71n4, 109, 109n3
wandering. See roaming
Wang Fuzhi, 49–51, 50n10–11
Wang Shizhen, 99–100, 99n21–3, 100n24
Wang Wei, 61, 61n5, 91, 91n9, 93, 97–99, 97n17–18, 98n20, 99n23
Wang Yangming, 117, 117n15
wind-light (*feng jing*), xi, 46–49, 52, 55, 66, 68, 85, 123. See also the perceptual
work (*travail*), xn6, 4, 4n6, 7, 59, 62, 71, 80–81, 102, 106
world, 12, 16, 18, 24–26, 38, 43–44, 48, 53, 55–61, 66, 68, 71–73, 78–79, 84–85, 87–88, 91, 93, 95–97, 99–101, 105–111, 113–20, 123–25; and breath energy (*qi*), 38, 115; Chinese apprehension of, 32, 61, 99–101,

117–18; and clearing out and opening up (*dégagement*), 56, 58, 99–100; coevality with landscape, 9; coevality with the self, 43; and connivance, 105, 107–10, 120; as Creation, 42; de-symbolizing/secularizing of, 28, 28n1; deployment of through pairing, 33; in Descartes, 117; and diversity/variety, 88; and emotion, 50; and the kiosk, 119–20; and Liberty, 123; in Mencius, 117; in Nietzsche, 109; non-metaphysicality of in Chinese thought, 31; non-overflowing of, 114; objectivation of, 53–54, 75, 106–7; outside of vs. inside of the soul, 14; in Plato, 49, 95; primordial coinvolvement of with the self, xn3, 108, 110, 114, 117, 124; as proceeding from polarities, 16, 26, 49–50; as process, 28–29, 118; as produced when a place becomes a link, 107, 109; and the self, 41, 45–46, 49, 51–52; spiritualization of, 52; in Wang Yangming, 117; worldness, 84–85, 108, 123; world-stuff, ix, 16, 18, 20, 24, 26, 28–19, 32–33, 38, 41, 43, 48; world-tension, 60, 74, 91, 108, 114–15; in Zhuangzi, 117;

Xie He, 29
Xie Lingyun, 22–23, 23n6, 30, 62, 86, 94, 96, 96n16
Xi Kang, 38, 97

yin and yang, 20–21, 34, 57, 60, 81, 89, 92
Yuan Mei, 120, 120n17

Zhang Dai, 96, 96n14
Zhang Zai, 57, 57n2
Zhuangzi (the *Zhuangzi*) (compilation), 99–100, 117, 120
Zong Bing, 58–60, 65

About the Author and Translator

François Jullien is Professor and Chair of the Department of Oriental Studies at Université de Paris-Diderot and Chair of Alterity at the Fondation Maison des Sciences de l'Homme. He is also president of the College International de Philosophie in Paris. His previous books on aesthetics, all translated into English, include *The Strange Idea of Beauty* (2015), *The Great Image Has No Form, or On the Nonobject Through Painting* (2009), and *The Impossible Nude* (2007).

Pedro Rodríguez is a writer and translator in the fields of fiction, history, science, philosophy, and business. He has received a Fulbright and an NEA grant (the latter for the translation of two novels and two travelogues by French-Cambodian writer George Groslier). He lives in Paris.

www.ingramcontent.com/pod-product-compliance
Lightning Source LLC
Chambersburg PA
CBHW020126240426
43673CB00038B/605